Fatal Identity
by
Gina Barton

Badger Books LLC
Middleton, Wisconsin, USA

ISBN: 9781932542363

Badger Books LLC
1600 N. High Point Rd.
Middleton, Wisconsin 53562, USA
Tel: 1-800-928-2372
Email: books@badgerbooks.com
Website: www.badgerbooks.com

This book is dedicated to the memory of Timothy Wicks

Acknowledgments

The author would like to thank her husband, Larry Barton, as well as the rest of her family for their love and support. Thanks also to Detective Kent Schoonover of the Hales Corners Police Department, Cass County State's Attorney Birch Burdick, and the others who lived this story for their assistance with this project.

PROLOGUE

A surveyor was the first to see the body. It sat just over the guardrail from the roadway, frozen, poised to plunge to the river below. There were smallish footprints — probably a woman's — among those in the fresh snow nearby.

As soon as the police saw the body, in January 2002, they knew they were looking for a killer, and a smart one at that. Dumping a dead man's body so close to the state line between Michigan's Upper Peninsula and northern Wisconsin was a perfect way to thwart an investigation. It meant detectives from at least two states would be running around in the subzero temperatures, trying to figure out who was in charge.

An even better way to make things rough for the cops was to make the body hard to identify. The killer had certainly done that. The victim had no clothes, no hands, and no head.

CHAPTER ONE

For Timothy Wicks, life was music — jazz music specifically. Dizzy Gillespie. Maynard Ferguson. Art Blakey. The sounds of his idols' recordings and his own practicing blasted from his Milwaukee-area apartments day and night, leading to his eviction from at least one. Jazz was Wicks' second religion. The drums were his instrument.

Wicks' father was an Episcopal deacon who had instilled a deep and introspective view of spirituality in his son. Even when the two grew apart years later, his father's lessons about religion, faith and the pursuit of God's plan remained with Wicks. He didn't see a conflict between his two passions. A bit of an evangelist, he sometimes handed out New Testaments to people he met over beers.

When Wicks wasn't drumming, he was reading. Besides books on religion and philosophy, he gravitated toward self-help manuals with titles such as "Think and Be Rich." He desperately hoped his drumming would one day lead to fortune. Fame wasn't quite as important. From his early days as a student at the Berklee School of Music in Boston, Wicks dreamed of making it big, at least big enough to avoid working for a living.

Wicks was realistic, though. He never completed his coursework at Berklee, perhaps because his creativity and discipline fell victim to his drug use. Drumming would be the best way to hit the jackpot, sure. But if that didn't work out, a windfall from some other source would be just fine. Money, no matter what its source, would allow him to quit his day job as a house painter and spend more time on his music.

Wicks' eclectic group of friends, many of them musicians or groupies, understood his little eccentricities. To strangers, his philosophical conversations could be distracting to the point of annoyance.

One of Wicks' oldest friends was Jim Koehler, whom he met in 1979. Koehler was between jobs as a factory worker in print shops, so he took a part-time position cooking at Captain's Steak Joint. Wicks was also a cook there.

Wicks eventually left the restaurant job to start his painting business. He preferred exterior painting with some small caulking jobs thrown in. He liked a schedule that wasn't 40 hours or even five days a week. To find jobs, he would cold call restaurants and businesses to ask if they needed painting done. He also put up notices on bulletin boards in grocery stores and other public places.

One night Wicks and Koehler walked several blocks from Wicks' suburban Milwaukee apartment to a neighborhood bar. Shortly after he ordered the beer on special, Wicks asked, "Hey, Jim, what's faster, an Indy car or a Lamborghini?"

Koehler didn't know and wasn't interested in the topic. He tried to change the subject. Wicks wouldn't quit, though.

"What's faster, an Indy car or a Lamborghini?" he asked over and over. "What's faster, an Indy car or a Lamborghini?"

"Well, I don't know, Tim," Koehler began.

Sometimes you had to humor Wicks. Just get the conversation over with and change the subject. This appeared to be one of those times. Koehler knew next to nothing about cars, but he tried to come up with something that would appease his friend, something about how an Indy car would probably be better under certain conditions, a Lamborghini under others.

The guy sitting beside the two friends just shook his head and muttered to Koehler, "That guy's crazy, man. Makes me want to kill him." He was speaking figuratively, Koehler was sure. If Wicks heard the comment, he didn't let on. Koehler led Wicks out of the bar just in case.

On another night, the two of them walked to Bon's Bar, another of Milwaukee's many neighborhood taverns. Wicks was in a strange mood. Not like he wanted to go out and fight somebody, but more aggressive than usual. In the parking lot, he pretended to throw bottles at cars, imitating the windup and pitch of a baseball player. He had a strange look on his face.

Then there were the times Wicks would drift off into his own zone, rubbing his hands together and muttering to himself, "Yeah. Yeah. Yeah. Yeah." Or the times he'd do Lamaze-type breathing exercises, though he'd never fathered a child. By the age of 48, he'd never married, and he didn't date much.

After leaving Boston and settling near Milwaukee in the late 1970s, Wicks continued his musical education at the Milwaukee Conservatory of Music. He practiced all the time. At one apartment in Milwaukee's Bay View neighborhood, a blue-collar area not far from Lake Michigan, Wicks had a huge living room that doubled as a music studio. The furniture was shabby, but the stereo system was state-of-the-art. Wicks' music collection was second to none. It included almost every venue and a range of artists from Grammy winners to virtual unknowns.

The living room was the perfect place for late-night jam sessions with his friends. Music often blared into the early morning hours. Eventually, the landlord kicked him out because of all the complaints about the noise.

At the bars, Wicks would sit in with whatever band would have him — and some that were just too polite to tell him to go away. He frequented open mike jams all over town. At one of them, Kokopelli's, he became a Sunday night fixture. The owner there befriended Wicks, and the regulars were disappointed on the rare occasions when he didn't show.

Bars where Wicks played regularly had a habit of going out of business, although no one could fault his drumming for that. At one of them, Sandy's National Pastime, Wicks' accountant, Dennis, was often in the audience. Wicks also played frequently at a bar called Rumors, but that establishment, like Sandy's, didn't last.

In contrast to the quirkiness of Wicks' personality, his playing was generally decent. The crowds seemed to approve. Between his various bands' sets at the bars near his home in the Milwaukee suburb of Hales Corners, Wicks would wedge himself into groups of women on the dance floor. Sometimes he moved in perfect rhythm to the recorded music piped over the sound system. Other times, he just tried to get as close as he could to the fans.

Wicks wasn't unattractive; he stood six feet tall and weighed about 185 pounds. His sandy blond hair, with just a touch of gray, was parted on the side and complemented his eyes.

When one of Wicks' bands got into a groove, there was no shortage of female fans throwing themselves and their telephone numbers his way. He'd display the numbers for his friends, but he never called the women. Koehler's wife, Judy, questioned whether Wicks might be gay. Wicks just didn't seem macho or manly enough to Judy. He struck her as almost childlike, with a naïve quality she considered feminine. Wicks never took offense. He just laughed off the insinuations.

Women were great, Wicks told his friends, but a commitment wasn't worth the trouble or the expense. A wife and kids would take time away from what mattered most, his music. A family also cost money and constrained your freedom. His freedom wasn't something Wicks was willing to give up lightly. Wicks never even wanted room-mates. He just didn't want the hassle.

For someone so concerned with wealth, Wicks didn't have many material possessions, nor did he seem to want them. For a while, he didn't even have a car. He was perfectly happy walking or taking the bus. Sometimes he bummed rides from his buddies.

No matter how a night started or where it ended, if Wicks was there, everyone had a good time. Even after more beers than he could count, he never got angry, never picked a fight. That isn't to say he was perfect. He did drink a bit too much sometimes.

Koehler worked the night shift, so even on his days off, he would sleep all day. Wicks would pick him up at 10 or 11 p.m., and the two would party until four or five in the morning.

They viewed drinking and driving a little differently. "Just give me two beers, and I'm done," Koehler would say.

"Drive straight and don't speed and you'll be okay," was Wicks' reply.

In December 2001, Wicks told his friends he was leaving Wisconsin, at least temporarily. He was headed to Canada with the guy who had done his taxes the year before, a fellow drummer named Dennis. The gig at a bar in Winnipeg would pay $800 a week — more money than Wicks had ever made performing, more than enough money to leave his paint rollers behind. More money than several friends and relatives felt he deserved, considering his middling talent.

When his friend from the Milwaukee Conservatory of Music, Bruce Sauter, asked for details, Wicks provided few. He wasn't even sure of the name of the place he would be playing. It was called Mirrors Pub or Mirrors Club, maybe Mirrors Pub Club, and it was in Winnipeg, Manitoba. Wicks planned to figure out the rest as he went along. As Wicks saw it, the mere possibility that the gig was as good as advertised was reason enough to take his shot.

Reasons to stay? There weren't many. Wicks only saw his sister, her husband, and their two daughters on holidays. Although they all loved each other, the brother and sister weren't particularly close. His odd personality sometimes drove Wicks' family to distraction. He had bouts of erratic behavior, which his brother-in-law suspected were due to dropping a lot of acid in his younger days. Either that or some undiagnosed mental illness.

By that time, Wicks' parents, who had started out as snowbirds, lived in Florida most of the year. Since their move, they had seen less and less of him. Wicks once complained to his friends that when his parents passed through Milwaukee on their annual summer jaunt to their cabin near Lake Superior in Ashland, Wisconsin — a vacation area the locals call "Up North" — they made it a point of dropping in on his sister, but never visited him.

His painting? That was easily put on hold. He finished the jobs he'd started and didn't make any effort to schedule new ones. If things didn't work out, he could always pick up where he'd left off.

Wicks decided to hang on to his apartment, just in case. The rent was affordable, the neighbors were okay, and the building manager, Stacey Paprocki, didn't give him flak about his practicing. Wicks promised Paprocki he would send the rent from Canada for a few months. Then he would either return and pack up the rest of his belongings or come back for good, depending on how things in Canada panned out.

Wicks didn't own a cell phone, nor did he know precisely where he would be staying once he reached Winnipeg. When Paprocki asked how she could contact him in case of emergency, he wrote Dennis' cell phone number on a scrap of paper. Even if he and Dennis didn't become roommates, they'd be playing together most nights. Dennis could always get him a message, Wicks told her.

On a cold day just after Christmas, Wicks and another man, a stocky guy of about 40, loaded Wicks' black and gray pearl Ludwig drums, Yamaha snare drum and Zildjian cymbals into his brand-new Chevy Cavalier — a black Z-24 he'd purchased just a few weeks before — and were gone.

After a couple of weeks, some of Wicks' friends started to worry because he hadn't checked in. While his family was used to Wicks' sporadic absences, his buddies from the Milwaukee music scene weren't. He'd promised them he would keep in touch. He knew they would be eager to hear how things were going once he got to Canada.

Sauter worried the most. Although Wicks said Dennis had frequented Sandy's National Pastime, Sauter had never met him, and apparently Dennis rarely socialized with others there. If Wicks knew Dennis' last name, he hadn't shared it with Sauter or any of his other friends. "A big guy with glasses who did peoples' taxes" was the sum total of information Sauter had about Wicks' new best friend.

Initially, it hadn't struck Sauter as odd that Wicks didn't know the exact name of the bar where he'd be playing. At the time, Sauter chalked it up to one of Wicks' brain freezes. Weeks after his friend's departure, Sauter wasn't so sure. He searched the Internet for Canadian bars that sounded like they could be the place. He called them all, but no one at any of them knew Wicks, nor did they know a drummer named Dennis. Sauter's concerns grew to the point of panic. He called the police.

*   *   *

The Hales Corners Police Department had a force of 17, and Kent Schoonover was the only detective. He led every investigation in town, from bad checks to the very rare murders. In 2002, the year Tim Wicks headed for Canada, there were 172 larcenies, no murders, and just one rape in Hales Corners, a village of 3.2 square miles located southwest of Milwaukee.

Schoonover worked a strange schedule — four days on, two days off — logged his share of holidays, and sometimes had to fill in on patrol when staffing got tight. Standing 6 feet 3 inches tall and weighing just over 300 pounds, Schoonover was an imposing figure with thinning brown hair and glasses.

He was incredibly camera shy and agreed to pose for only a single photograph at his own wedding, a plan his wife was well aware of when she agreed to marry him. Forced to pose for a police department picture, he slouched in the back row. The chief's plans to display the photo in the lobby were ruined because Schoonover's face was obscured by the man in front of him.

Schoonover, who got his first part-time police job in 1977, said he chose a career in law enforcement to help people, even though he knew that was a cliché. He was the lead instructor at the Hales Corners Citizens' Police Academy and was happy to take calls from any of the town's 7,740 residents. Many were impressed with his straightforward manner and had called on him personally more than once. Most of the time, Schoonover's cases had positive results. Stolen property was recovered. A burglar was caught. An abusive husband was arrested.

Schoonover loved his job despite the huge amounts of paperwork it included. He didn't even mind dealing with the Milwaukee County district attorney's office. The super-educated big city lawyers always made sure he was kept up to date on the status of prosecutions. Schoonover was convinced the local prosecutors valued his cooperation and considered him a true partner in the justice system.

To Schoonover, the officers of the Hales Corners Police Department weren't quite a brotherhood, since there were two women on the force. They were, however, a family. Schoonover knew his cases didn't get solved in a vacuum. The officers on the street were his backup and his colleagues. All of them deserved the same courtesy and credit he received from the chief. A detective division of one, Schoonover often turned to his subordinates for brainstorming on difficult cases, moral support and camaraderie. The fact that he sometimes went out on patrol helped him seem more like one of them. He never felt a ride in the squad was beneath him, and he took the same care writing a traffic ticket as he did working a crime scene.

When Bruce Sauter first called about his missing friend, Timothy Wicks, Schoonover wasn't the least bit worried. Sauter seemed a bit of an odd duck, unsophisticated and inarticulate. More than likely, he was overreacting.

Besides, Hales Corners was nothing like nearby Milwaukee, where murders and shootings were almost daily occurrences. The inner-city gangs hadn't made their way far enough west to be much of a problem in the suburbs. Random violence was almost unheard of on the streets of Hales Corners, and Sauter himself said Wicks didn't have any enemies. In fact, when Schoonover contacted Wicks' family, they told him about Wicks' proclivity for being out of touch for months at a time. He was a free spirit who wanted to experience all the world had to offer. He'd even traveled to neighboring Illinois once or twice in the past for what had sounded like promising music jobs.

In Schoonover's view, failing to call friends wasn't a crime, nor was it a reason to panic, no matter what Sauter thought. Schoonover had absolutely no reason to fear that something horrible had happened to Sauter's friend. Wicks, a grown man, had the right to disappear if he wanted to. Schoonover had to prioritize.

CHAPTER TWO

Jim Koehler first heard about his friend's potential drumming gig as the two drank beers at a neighborhood tavern called Victor's in March 2001. "You can always try it out," Koehler recalls saying.

Wicks added, "Yeah, if it doesn't work out, I can always come back."

By fall, the plan seemed to be getting closer to reality. One November day, Wicks phoned Dave Deruyter, owner of the Red Mill West, a music club where Wicks was sometimes invited to sit in as a drummer. Deruyter considered Wicks an average drummer, so he was surprised when Wicks asked to use the club's recording studio. "I've got this job offer in Canada, and I've got to send out a demo tape with a couple of songs," Wicks told Deruyter.

November rolled into December, and Wicks spent the early part of Christmas Eve with another friend, Gerry Boettcher, and Boettcher's mother. He then stopped to see his own family. Wicks invited his brother-in-law, Tom Neary, outside to see his new Cavalier. Neary wasn't particularly interested in Wicks' new car, but he wanted to be sure his brother-in-law could drive. Neary had never seen Wicks operate a car. The two men got into the Cavalier and cruised around the snow-covered block as Wicks shared the news of the drumming job.

"Tim, this guy is bullshiting you," Neary remembers saying. "There's no way you're going to get $800 a week. They don't even pay that in New Orleans."

Neary knew what he was talking about. An avid guitar player, his parents had let him wander Europe, playing in bands, when he was young. He had recorded albums in Nashville and New York. This Winnipeg thing just didn't seem right to him. Neary hoped he was wrong, but he had a feeling Wicks would come back home with his tail between his legs like a hurt puppy.

11

Wicks brushed off his brother-in-law's concerns. "Maybe things are different in Canada," Wicks told Neary. "Maybe Canadians appreciate live blues more than Americans. Maybe jobs pay better there."

In the end, Neary remained skeptical, but hugged Wicks and wished him luck.

Back in the house, Wicks told his family that Dennis had instructed him to keep their plans for Canada a secret. Neary thought that was odd. It hadn't been a secret before, and Wicks didn't know why things had changed. Wicks was unconcerned, however, so Neary didn't push it.

"I don't want him to go," Wicks' mother, Fay, told the others.

"Mom, he's 48 years old, for Chrissake. Of course he's going to go," Neary told her.

"Why is this a secret, Tim?" Fay kept asking her son.

"Dennis wants it to be a secret," he answered.

"Why?" she badgered him. "Why does Dennis want it to be a secret?"

Her son just shrugged. "I'll send you a post card," Wicks told his family before heading off into the night.

Around midnight, Wicks and Koehler hit the bars one last time.

"Well, I'm really going to Manitoba," Wicks told his friend.

"Geez, it's pretty cold up there," Koehler responded.

Wicks told Koehler a bit more about his plans and about Dennis, his fellow musician. Dennis had a house, Wicks told Koehler. Wicks would stay there, at least until he figured out a more permanent plan.

Koehler started thinking maybe this Dennis guy was a homosexual. Koehler's wife had entertained the same thought about Wicks, and Koehler supposed anything was possible. Koehler couldn't see any other reason Dennis would want another guy to move in with him.

12

"Is he gay?" Koehler asked.

Wicks laughed at the idea. "He's got a wife," he told Koehler.

That set Koehler's mind at ease.

The next day, Wicks called his mother and told her he was on his way up north to Canada. She never heard from him again.

*   *   *

Sgt. Greg Tamlyn of the Michigan State Police got the call about the headless body around 2:30 p.m. on January 2, 2002. Tamlyn cringed when Trooper Ron Marker described the location, County Road 374 near the Nathan Bridge in Menominee County's Holmes Township. In Tamlyn's five years as a detective, there had been only two homicides in the county of about 25,000 residents. The body on the bridge made three, and its location was eerily familiar. Three years before, about 200 or 300 yards away, the police had dug up the remains of Thomas Pohl, a contractor from Wheeling, Illinois. Pohl had been missing for five months. He and his killer had taken several hunting and fishing trips to the rural area near the river.

Tamlyn feared history was repeating itself as he gazed at the latest crime scene. The nude body, a man's, was sitting on the high bank of the Menominee River as if it had been carelessly tossed over the guardrail. The six inches of snow on the ground nearby were virgin white. Snowflakes were still falling, filling in the surrounding footprints more and more with each passing minute. The air temperature was 21 degrees and falling. There wasn't much blood at the scene, just a smear on the rail. On the body itself, the stump of a neck was crimson, with a bit of dried grass stuck to it, and blood had dripped onto the right shoulder.

The arms were bent, as if the man's hands had been near his face when they were severed. But instead of hands,

13

only smooth, clean wrists remained. There was a single cut on the chest, as if a saw had sliced completely through the man's left wrist and proceeded to the skin below. The cuts to the wrists were precise and neat, with no signs that the veins and arteries had been severed while life still pumped through them. Tamlyn deduced that all of the cuts had been made postmortem, and the body very well might have been frozen solid at the time. Marks near the armpits told Tamlyn that perhaps the man's assailant had threaded a rope under his arms and dragged him across the snow.

Tamlyn instructed officers to ring the area with crime scene tape and ordered the bridge closed to all traffic, blocking the two-lane road from Michigan's Upper Peninsula into Wisconsin.

Michigan's Upper Peninsula is separated from the rest of the state by the lake of the same name. Lake Superior borders the area to the west. On a map, the U.P., as the locals call it, is directly north of the state of Wisconsin. In addition to being geographically isolated from the rest of Michigan, the U.P. contains only about four percent of the state's ten million people. On that winter day in January 2002, both factors were a problem for Tamlyn.

When Tamlyn called for a team to gather forensic evidence, he learned that the single crew assigned to homicides in the region was already investigating a likely murder/suicide in Sini, about a three-hour drive from the Nathan Bridge. The team couldn't leave any time soon. They needed to finish processing the Sini scene.

Tamlyn next called the state crime lab in Grayling, in lower Michigan. Officials there estimated it would take about five hours to get to Tamlyn's scene and a minimum of 12 hours to process it. There would be no way to do their work effectively after sunset. Instead, they promised to get on the road at 4 a.m. in order to get to the riverbank by daylight. A state police officer stood guard through the cold, snowy night as the mercury dipped to 9 degrees.

14

By twilight the following day, the crime lab technicians had finished their work at the scene. Gary Anderson of Anderson-Diehm Funeral Home removed the frozen body. The authorities agreed to leave the body in the hearse in the hopes that it would begin to thaw. The hearse, under guard, was parked overnight in the garage at the state police post.

Tamlyn wanted a forensic pathologist — someone with actual medical training rather than a layperson elected coroner — and an autopsy. The nearest Michigan pathologist was in Grand Rapids, about 450 miles away. Instead, the authorities decided to take the headless John Doe to Milwaukee, which was closer.

On Friday, Tamlyn drove the body 175 miles to Milwaukee, where he was told it was still too frozen for autopsy. The body was placed in a 40-degree cooler where it could warm up gradually.

While the body thawed, Tamlyn dispatched a state police K-9 team to the Nathan Bridge in hopes that the dogs would sniff out additional evidence. There was none.

One trooper issued press releases, hoping to generate tips about the corpse's identity or how it had come to end up on the riverbank.

Dr. Alan K. Stormo, an assistant medical examiner in Milwaukee, finally conducted the autopsy five days after the body was discovered. He determined that the victim was most likely a smoker and probably had not worked with his hands.

As Tamlyn had suspected, the cuts to the neck and wrists had been made after death. The cause of death, though, could not be determined. Stormo also couldn't determine the time of death because the body had been frozen. There were blue fibers on the body, perhaps from a carpet or a blanket, but they were useless without something to compare them to.

Tamlyn realized that with no head and no hands, the only possible way to identify the corpse was through DNA.

That test also couldn't be done without a known sample for comparison. The body was the needle; all the reports of missing people in the region were the haystack.

Tamlyn sent out a notice informing other departments about the body. Maybe one of them would have a missing person's report that matched the corpse's vital statistics: height, 6'1" to 6'3"; age, 40 to 50; weight, 185 to 200 pounds; fair complexion; possibly red hair; and a 9 ¾ foot size. Tamlyn had been hoping for scars, tattoos, or some other distinguishing characteristics, but there were none. He sent the bulletin to 13 surrounding states and set up a tip line, but he wasn't optimistic.

CHAPTER THREE

Gardner, North Dakota, population 85, would make a great place to disappear. The town's main thoroughfare is paved with gravel. The volunteer fire department raises funds with an annual smelt fry. A grain elevator, the most visible landmark in town, overshadows everything, as does the unmuffled traffic noise of Interstate Highway 29.

The small white box of a building on the corner of Front and 4th streets is the post office. In November 2001, two months before the frozen torso was found near the Wisconsin-Michigan border, the old blue farmhouse across the street became the home of a man calling himself Tim Wicks, his wife, Diana, and her son, Joshua. After the family completed their move from a rented duplex in nearby Fargo, the man went to the Spherion employment agency in search of a job.

Gene Maxwell and Jeff Paridon's small start-up company in Fargo had been in business less than a year, but already they had gone through several bookkeepers. The latest bookkeeper at Compressed Air Technologies had abruptly moved to Wyoming. The front desk sat empty. No one was there to greet customers or pay the bills. The fledgling business, which sold and serviced industrial air compressors, was in jeopardy.

Originally Maxwell and Paridon figured they would make a great team. All kinds of businesses needed air compressors for operating hand tools, powering factory equipment, sand blasting and spray painting. Paridon was the salesman, on the road in North Dakota and neighboring Minnesota soliciting clients in the automotive, agricultural, and manufacturing industries, just to name a few. Maxwell got the administrative side of the business going, and then switched to the business manager's post. He also served as a repairman and was adept at fixing assorted brands of compressors.

However, the two men had underestimated the difficulty they would have finding good help. Their vision for their dream venture had included a reliable, hard-working employee who would run the office, leaving the cofounders free to grow the business. In fact, the business was already growing, from just the two of them when they started to eight by the time their second bookkeeper left.

Maxwell and Paridon were optimistic they would succeed working for themselves, but they felt it was important to find the right person for the bookkeeper's job, someone knowledgeable and trustworthy. Unsure of how to recruit a candidate or how to conduct an effective background investigation, they had turned to Spherion. By November 2001, the agency hadn't sent anyone suitable, and Maxwell and Paridon were growing impatient. Paridon made their frustrations known, telling the people at the agency they would have to come up with someone soon. Spherion responded by giving Paridon and his partner the résumé of Tim Wicks.

On paper, Wicks seemed the ideal man for the job. His résumé listed experience and education in both Wisconsin and Manitoba. The man's objective, according to the résumé, was "To secure a position offering challenge, accountability, and an opportunity for advancement." Compressed Air could certainly offer him that. In addition to proficiency in several computer programs, the résumé touted Wicks' specialized experience: analyzing accounts and conducting fraud investigations at the Zoological Society of Manitoba; bookkeeping for 40 clients simultaneously at Lodis Financial Group in Milwaukee; and acting as "role model and mentor" for new employees at several different companies.

According to his Spherion application, Wicks hoped to earn $12 an hour and was willing to work any time between 6 a.m. and midnight. He was willing to do only medium lifting and preferred a non-smoking environment. (Paridon and Maxwell hoped the guy needed a job enough

18

to get past that one. In their office, everyone lit up right at their desks.)

In answer to the question, "Have you ever been convicted of a felony, misdemeanor or any offense other than a minor traffic violation?" Wicks had checked the box marked "no."

Asked to describe a challenge faced in a work situation, the applicant wrote: "Detected fraud situation performed by another accounting firm including criminal activity. I confronted the client and the problem was resolved legally."

The Spherion interviewer rated the candidate with repeated superlatives. He was very outgoing, very cooperative, very articulate, very professional and well-informed. On a software test, he achieved an overall score of 80 percent.

Maxwell and Paridon decided to give Wicks a try. They liked him immediately. He blended well into their office, where all the workers were on a first-name basis. He seemed glad to have the job and the health insurance that covered treatment for his diabetes. Wicks' responsibilities included completing the payroll, making sure the taxes were up-to-date, and paying the bills.

Wicks seemed trustworthy, well-educated and professional. He quickly gained his employers' confidence. He had a positive attitude, laughing and joking with the others in the office. Maxwell and Paridon recall thinking many times, "This guy is good for us." They were grateful the agency had sent them not only a well-qualified employee, but also someone who could help take their new business to the next level. Wicks was well worth the fee they'd paid the agency, a bargain. "We've finally found the person we needed for the position," Paridon told several people. "I can finally concentrate on the job I do best: sales."

In a relatively short time, Wicks and Maxwell forged a friendship. In office conversation, Maxwell told Wicks he had bought a new scope for his deer hunting rifle.

Maxwell had planned to take the scope into a shop and have it professionally mounted on the rifle. Wicks explained that he was somewhat of a weapons enthusiast. "I'll do it for you," he offered.

The last weekend of the deer hunting season, Maxwell and Wicks tested the scope. It worked perfectly. Wicks mentioned some property he owned in Michigan's Upper Peninsula. He also talked about his gun collection, which included quite a few vintage firearms inherited from his father.

Maxwell did the sort of favors for Wicks he would do for any other friend. In November, when Wicks bought the house in Gardner, about 30 miles north of Fargo, Maxwell helped him move a gas stove into the kitchen. A short time later, Wicks had a problem with his new washing machine and feared it had not been installed properly. Sure enough, Maxwell recognized that the machine's drain hose was too long, and he easily shortened it. After Maxwell attached the modified hose, Wicks and his wife, Diana, insisted he stay for dinner with them. Over pizza and beers, they whiled away a pleasant evening.

Paridon lived 85 miles across the Minnesota border, so he had less time to socialize with co-workers. But because Wicks was such a good employee, and because Maxwell liked him so much, Paridon was willing to help Wicks on occasion. Shortly after Wicks moved into his new house, he asked Paridon to stop by and take a look at a foundation problem in the basement.

Paridon, who spent most of his time on the road making sales calls, stopped in Gardner one evening at the end of his workday. He noted that the walls of the poured concrete basement were buckling pretty good and starting to crack. Paridon told Wicks the problem could be fixed, but it would take some work. The area surrounding the house needed excavating outside with a Bobcat or some other small backhoe. Then Wicks would have to pour gravel and lay drain tile to carry water away from the house's foundation.

Paridon and Maxwell found Wicks' wife pleasant but not particularly talkative. Wicks had told both bosses about her problems with alcohol and with her son's father. Sometime after Paridon visited the house, Wicks asked his boss to give his wife a loan to pay her lawyer in a child custody dispute. Paridon gave Diana a check for $600 and said she could pay it back by helping her husband do office work.

Wicks' wife worked only one day each week. She was quiet and withdrawn. Paridon and Maxwell questioned how much work she actually did, but they didn't address the issue. Wicks did such a good job for them, they were willing to forgive a minor problem with the wife.

Wicks and Paridon also had music in common. One night Paridon invited Wicks to play a set with his band. Wicks showed up and played the drums, but not very well. Paridon suspected he'd never had formal training, but he sure seemed to love drumming.

About four months after the new guy started, Maxwell noticed some unusual entries in the company's books. They were things that come up often enough in a small business: What cost $50 at Office Depot? Why were there checks made out to petty cash? Maxwell fully expected the man running his office to offer an innocent explanation that could be documented and forgotten. When he questioned Wicks, though, he received an answer along the lines of, "I don't know. I'll get back to you." But the bookkeeper never did.

Although Compressed Air was open for business on Christmas Eve, Wicks didn't come to work that day. One morning later in the week, he showed up looking for his check. Paridon, who stopped by the office briefly before going out on sales calls, noticed Diana and another man waiting outside in a car he'd never seen before. The car was sporty and black, and it had Wisconsin plates. Paridon spoke to Wicks in passing, then went inside to attend to his work. By the time he had finished at his desk, Wicks, his wife, and the stranger were gone.

About a week later, Wicks called Paridon at home and asked if he could borrow one of the company trucks to haul a Bobcat. Paridon refused. Compressed Air offered service 24 hours a day, seven days a week. If a client needed a repair and the truck wasn't at the shop, the job couldn't get done in a timely manner. The customer had to come first. Paridon vaguely wondered why Wicks needed a Bobcat in the middle of winter. The ground outside was frozen solid, definitely not a good time for Wicks to be working on his basement problem.

With or without his boss' permission, it would have been easy for Wicks to take the truck. Maxwell, out on service calls, and Paridon, out on sales calls, were rarely there. Wicks had a set of keys to the office, and the keys to the company vehicles were hanging inside.

After that phone call, Paridon fully expected Wicks to show up for work on January 2. When he didn't, Paridon worried. The Gardner house was an old one. Maybe there was a problem with the furnace leaking carbon monoxide. Maybe Wicks had slipped into a diabetic coma. Maybe his wife's ex had shown up and caused trouble.

Paridon called Wicks several times, but couldn't reach him at home or on his cell phone. Paridon drove out to the house, and the scene there seemed to confirm his fears. No one answered his knock. Paridon went back to his truck, which was parked in the driveway, and called the house from his cell phone as he watched the door. No one answered.

Two cars were parked outside, the dark blue Buick with North Dakota plates that Wicks usually drove to work and the black sports car, a Cavalier Z-24. Neither vehicle looked as if it had been moved in quite some time. Paridon felt uneasy. He pulled out his cell phone again. This time, he called the sheriff's department.

Cass County Sheriff's deputies Patricia Wasmuth and Bruce Renshaw had been on patrol in the area and arrived a short time later. Paridon was sitting in his truck, waiting for them. Wasmuth, a sheriff's deputy for 20 years, knocked on the door of the blue farmhouse. No answer. She tried to turn the knob, but the door was locked. The two deputies looked in the windows but saw no one. Wasmuth called her supervisor and asked for permission to break in. Then, she called the fire department to help with the task. She had hoped they could gain entry to the premises without causing any damage. Unfortunately, the door broke as the firefighters pried it open.

Wasmuth's first thought upon entering was that the place certainly looked lived in. The Christmas tree stood tall in the living room, and toys were scattered on the floor. In the kitchen, pots and pans sat on the stove. Blood from a roast or some other cut of meat stained the top of the stove and the inside of the refrigerator. In the bedrooms, clothes littered the floors. Beds were unmade. Wasmuth thumbed through a stack of mail on a table and noticed a cosmetology license from Wisconsin among the envelopes.

No one was home. There was no sign of where the home's occupants had gone, and no sign they had met with foul play.

Wasmuth placed a note for the family on the stove. She wanted to be sure they would see it when they got home, so they wouldn't be alarmed by the damaged door.

The note read: "Tim Wicks, Sheriff's Dept. was here on a welfare check — your boss has not heard from you. We were concerned for your health and safety. We were required to break the door. Please contact our office regarding your safety. Thank you, Cass County Sheriff's Department."

Wasmuth instructed the firefighters to close the door as best they could. She told Paridon no one was home. Then she noted the license plate numbers of the two vehicles outside. Later, back at the office, she ran the plates.

23

The blue Buick was registered to one Hazel Gaede, reportedly of Enderlin, North Dakota. The black Chevy with Wisconsin plates was registered to Timothy W. Wicks of Hales Corners, Wisconsin.

Paridon was baffled. Things were starting to fall apart at work. They were trying to operate without their bookkeeper, office manager and all around Guy Friday. When they tried to do some of the work themselves, they realized Wicks had changed all of the pass codes for their computers. They could no longer get into their own company's systems.

In response to Paridon's many messages, Wicks finally called back with a muddled explanation for his absence. He and his wife had gone down to Tijuana with some friends, gotten too drunk, gotten into some trouble and been arrested, Wicks said. They were en route back to Fargo and were at that very minute driving through Ohio, he assured his boss.

Instead of making Paridon feel better, the call made him more nervous. Tijuana was across the California border from the United States, thousands of miles west of Fargo. If Wicks was really coming home from there, why would he be in Ohio, some 1,200 miles to the east? Paridon was starting to get the sinking feeling that he had been conned. Maxwell could have kicked himself for not questioning the bookkeeper more thoroughly about those seemingly innocent entries in the ledgers.

Maxwell and Paridon decided to dig more deeply into their company's financial records. The more they looked, the more trouble they found.

*   *   *

Tammy Lynk was the sole investigator for the Fargo Police Department's District Three. When Lynk received a phone call about a possible embezzlement at Compressed Air Technologies, she added it to her ever-

24

growing list of things to do. She told Maxwell and Paridon to call her the next time Wicks was in the office so she could come and talk to him. Maxwell wasn't optimistic. "We'll never see him again," he thought. "No way would he be stupid enough to come back here."

On January 7, Paridon reached Wicks by phone and literally begged him to come back to work. "We really need the access codes for the computers," Paridon pleaded.

To Maxwell's disbelief, Wicks, driving the black Z-24 Chevy Cavalier, showed up for work later that morning. Paridon asked him about the car, and Wicks said he'd just bought it. Paridon figured it had probably been purchased with the proceeds of the theft from his company. Neither Maxwell nor Paridon wanted to arouse Wicks' suspicions, so they pretended to believe his tale about the trip to Tijuana. As soon as Maxwell had the opportunity, he stole into his office and dialed Tammy Lynk, telling her Wicks had returned.

Lynk couldn't immediately head for Compressed Air. She'd recently had surgery on both knees and couldn't drive. She told Maxwell she would try to get a ride.

Meanwhile, Paridon grabbed a Polaroid camera and snapped Wicks' picture, telling him it was for a company bulletin board. Wicks posed and smiled, but by the time the two owners got back from lunch that day, the bookkeeper had cleaned out his desk and left. He phoned later, saying he was sick.

By that time, Lynk had arranged her transportation. Knowing she had missed Wicks at the office, she headed for his farmhouse in Gardner. Sitting in the driveway, waiting for Wicks to show up, Lynk used her cell phone to reach Wicks on his. Surprisingly, he answered, and he didn't hang up when Lynk told him she was the police.

"We need to talk to you about a theft," she remembers telling him.

The bookkeeper sounded almost relieved. He calmly explained that Lynk had it all wrong. He wasn't the one embezzling. It was Maxwell and Paridon who had been cooking the books long before Wicks was hired. They were guilty of tax evasion, and maybe even criminal fraud, the man said. When he'd confronted his bosses about it, they threatened to put the blame on him, he told Lynk. He had the documentation to prove they were lying, and he wouldn't let them get away with it. Wicks agreed to come to the police station in a few days to show Lynk his proof.

The next day, Wicks called Maxwell and resigned from his job at Compressed Air. He wouldn't be coming back to work, Wicks said, because Paridon was making it an unfriendly environment for him.

CHAPTER FOUR

The discovery of a headless body with no hands on the shores of the Menominee River didn't stop workers from the U.S. Geological Survey from returning to their duties in the area of the Nathan Bridge.

About two weeks after the body was found, 17 miles upriver, another surveyor rowed along, searching for a promising place to mine for precious metals. Although the temperature was below zero on that day — January 16, 2002 — the shallow water was so close to a dam that its constant flow kept it from freezing.

Something on the river bottom caught the surveyor's eye. He wasn't sure what it was until he prodded it with an oar. Then he realized the awful truth. He was looking at a human head.

Since the head was on the Wisconsin side of the river, the crime scene was technically outside Sgt. Greg Tamlyn's Michigan jurisdiction. He went anyway. He was sure the recently discovered head and the body from a couple of weeks before were a matched set. That gave the police a bit more to go on, but the guy was still a John Doe.

Tamlyn called the Milwaukee medical examiner's office, and the pathologist who had examined the body told him to put the head in a five-gallon bucket of ice and bring it down the following day. Fish had found the head before the police did, and it was barely recognizable. On the left side was a small hole. Lodged inside was a bullet.

Back in Hales Corners, Tim Wicks' friends kept nagging the police. Bruce Sauter wanted almost constant updates. Gerry Boettcher, who had last seen Wicks late on Christmas Eve, also was growing concerned. Schoonover decided it would be relatively easy to help them. He could track down Wicks, tell him to call his buddies, and that would be that.

Although his family hadn't heard from Wicks for two weeks, only his mother was concerned. To Beth and

27

Tom Neary, Wicks' lack of communication was normal. Even when they learned that his friends had reported him missing, nobody panicked.

"Don't worry, he'll call," Neary reassured his mother-in-law after a police sergeant called from Hales Corners, asking if the family had heard from Wicks. "He's with somebody. He'll be okay."

Schoonover turned to the resident manager at the Parkside Apartments, where Wicks had been living. Stacey Paprocki told Schoonover she had last spoken with Wicks on Christmas, when he knocked on her door and handed her his rent check.

"He told me he was going on a trip. He and a friend were going up to Canada. They were doing a band gig," Paprocki later recalled. "He was pretty excited about it."

Wicks had told Paprocki he might have to mail the February rent, she told Schoonover. Then Wicks had pulled out a square of paper and written down a number where she could reach him if anything went wrong with the apartment. The next day, Paprocki saw Wicks one last time, as he loaded his drums into his new Z-24 Cavalier. When Schoonover spoke with Paprocki, she still had the card, which read: "Dennis + Tim Wicks 1-701-799-0895."

Schoonover and Officer Gary Lindenlaub went through Wicks' apartment, looking for some trace of the "fat accountant named Dennis" that Sauter had described. The apartment didn't look like its occupant had left town. Clothes were draped across furniture. There wasn't much empty space in the closets. One of them overflowed with books on religion. The bathroom was full of toiletry items. The rest of the place contained books, records, compact discs, and religious items. Documents in the apartment indicated that Wicks was in the process of buying real estate of some kind.

It wasn't hard to find Wicks' tax returns. The preparer's signature was illegible, but the social security number beside it had been issued to a man named Dennis

Gaede. Next, Schoonover ran a motor vehicle check on Wicks. The detective found out that Wicks' Wisconsin driver's license was no longer valid. He'd apparently traded it in for a new one in North Dakota.

Later that day, Sgt. Richard Pawlak, who was assisting Schoonover and Lindenlaub in the investigation, called the number Wicks left with Paprocki, but got no answer. The voice mail was full, so he couldn't leave a message.

A few days later, Pawlak again dialed the contact number Wicks had left behind. This time, a man answered and said his name was Dennis Johnson, he lived at 1123 S. Third Street in Bismarck, North Dakota, and he didn't know any Tim Wicks.

With that, Schoonover's priorities began to change. He took the reins back from Pawlak and called the Bismarck police for help tracing the address and phone number. As it turned out, there was no 1123 South Third Street in Bismarck. There was a 123 South Third Street, but an elderly woman lived there.

The phone number, the Bismarck Police told Schoonover, had a Fargo prefix. Schoonover's call to the police department there was transferred to Investigator Tammy Lynk. He told her he was looking for information on a man named Dennis Gaede. Lynk had never heard of him. Schoonover was about to hang up. As an afterthought, he asked, "How about Timothy Wicks?"

Lynk thought the question was strange. Wicks wasn't missing, she told the detective from Wisconsin. She had been investigating him after receiving a fraud complaint from his employer, Compressed Air Technologies. He was scheduled to meet her at the Fargo police station that afternoon.

Schoonover could have left it at that. Wicks had simply moved without telling his friends. Missing person's case solved. But he didn't. Instead Schoonover asked Lynk to describe her Timothy Wicks. About 6 feet 3 inches tall, she said, recalling the Polaroid photo. Three hundred twenty-five pounds. Balding. Wears glasses.

While investigating Wicks' disappearance, Schoonover had seen several photos of the missing man, and Lynk's description didn't sound anything like him. It sounded familiar, though. Even before faxed photos from the Department of Motor Vehicles confirmed it, Schoonover knew. He had no doubt that Lynk was describing Gaede — who apparently was using Wicks' name.

But neither cop could answer the question that was becoming more and more troubling. What had happened to the real Timothy Wicks?

Lynk figured she would have all the answers later that day, when Compressed Air's accountant came to the station for his interview. He had promised to bring proof of Paridon and Maxwell's purported crimes.

Lynk was genuinely surprised when the accountant didn't show up, her odd conversation with Schoonover notwithstanding. When she couldn't reach the bookkeeper by phone, Lynk turned to Compressed Air's checkbook, hoping it would yield some answers. There were plenty of questionable entries, including one for a $600 check to cash that had been payable to a woman named Diana Fruge. Another check, Number 5107, had been made payable to Randy R. Rick. Lynk tracked down Rick, who turned out to be a landlord.

"Do you know a man by the name of Timothy Wicks?" Lynk asked him.

Rick hesitated. The name sounded familiar, he said, but he wasn't sure quite why. Then it came to him. One of his renters had used the name Tim Wicks, although that wasn't the name on the lease. Rick said the man, whose real name he couldn't recall, and the man's wife had rented the lower floor of a duplex at 1123 South Third Street. A young boy had also stayed with them. The $400 check was equivalent to one month's rent.

The landlord's wife, Gloria Rick, told Lynk that Dennis Gaede and his wife, Diana Gaede, had rented the apartment. Gloria Rick remembered some strange things about the couple. For example, when she received calls from their apartment, the name on the Caller ID was Tim Wicks. For a time, there had been three names on the mailbox: Wicks, Gaede and Fruge. Gloria Rick remembered calling Diana once at her workplace, Camelot Cleaners. The person who answered the phone said no one by the name of Diana Gaede worked there, but they did have a Diana Fruge. Fruge came to the phone, and turned out to be the Ricks' tenant using a different name.

Gloria Rick further told Lynk that she had never received the December rent check drawn on Compressed Air's account. The Gaedes skipped out without paying that month's rent, and she hadn't seen them since, Gloria Rick said.

Lynk was growing more and more confused. Why was Diana using two different names? Had Wicks lived with the Gaedes for a time? If Dennis Gaede was posing as Tim Wicks, why would he put his real name on the mailbox?

Lynk next interviewed some of the accountant's co-workers at Compressed Air. Justin Yagow, who worked in the parts department, offered a few interesting tidbits that Lynk wasn't sure were relevant — or even true. Yagow had once talked with the man he knew as Wicks about buying a motorcycle. During the conversation, the bookkeeper said that he was affiliated with the Hell's Angels motorcycle gang. Pressed for details, he added that his family back in Milwaukee had ties to the mob.

CHAPTER FIVE

After his conversation with Lynk, Schoonover got the feeling things had ended badly for Wicks. The most likely scenario seemed to be that Wicks was dead, and Gaede killed him. But how could Schoonover figure that out for sure? What was the next step?

In missing persons' cases, one of law enforcement's most valuable tools is the FBI's National Criminal Information Center, a database known in cop parlance as NCIC. Any missing child can be entered into the system. Adults, though, are allowed to disappear if they want to. Officers may only list a missing adult in the database if they have probable cause to believe the person is in danger or didn't voluntarily disappear. Once the case has become part of the system, the officer can check any number of reports, including lists of known gang members and terrorists, descriptions of stolen guns, criminal history records and motor vehicle records. Federal agents audit the system often, and local departments that stretch the rules risk banishment from the database.

Schoonover had little more than his intuition to support the theory that Wicks was in danger. It was probably premature to list him as "endangered missing" on the national database, but on January 19, 2002, Schoonover did it anyway.

The gamble paid off. Schoonover noticed almost immediately that the police in Franklin, a suburb less than five miles from Hales Corners, had run Wicks' plates four times in the past five days. No arrests had been made and no tickets were issued. Schoonover called his counterparts in the neighboring town. He was told that the black Z-24 had been spotted at the Park Motel, off 76th Street near the airport.

If suburban Milwaukee had a red light district, the Park Motel was in it. Officers were suspicious because the Cavalier was in the middle of the parking lot rather than in front of a particular unit. They suspected its owner, a 6-foot, 250-pound man with glasses, was meeting prostitutes.

Schoonover headed to the motel, where a desk clerk told him Timothy Wicks' room was paid for through January 22. A woman had registered and paid cash, the clerk said. The woman and her husband had recently purchased an RV, the clerk said, and they planned to travel the country in it.

The clerk gave Schoonover a key, and he entered the motel room.

*   *   *

The woman who came into the showroom at Hall Chevrolet seemed nervous. She abruptly handed a set of Cavalier keys to a salesman, Dino Echevarria.

"My boyfriend can't afford the payments anymore," she said. "He was too embarrassed to come in himself." The woman pointed to where the car was parked, then turned and hightailed it out the door.

Echevarria went after her. Customers couldn't just drop off cars like that. There was paperwork that had to be done. If her boyfriend didn't complete it, he would still be on the hook for the payments. The car would have to be considered abandoned. The salesman tried to explain the situation to the woman's back as she walked toward the street, but she didn't turn.

The car had no plates, but it seemed in good shape otherwise. Echevarria reported the incident to his manager, Shannon Fluhr. Two days later, Fluhr answered a telephone call from Pawlak of the Hales Corners Police. The officer had been assigned to call all the Chevy dealerships in the area, looking for information about Wicks' purchase of a Z-24 and the status of his payments.

Fluhr told Pawlak that not only had he sold Wicks the car, he now had it back on the lot. Pawlak, in turn, immediately dialed Schoonover's cell phone.

34

When the call came in, Schoonover was standing in the room registered to Wicks at the Park Motel. There were a few empty suitcases, fast food wrappers, and other garbage, but it was pretty clear the occupants weren't coming back.

Schoonover called a tow truck and headed for the auto dealership, hopeful that the car would contain fingerprints or some other evidence linking it to Gaede.

Echevarria described the woman who had dropped off the car as "big boned," with brown hair and blue eyes. She gave him the keys with her right hand, the salesman said. In her left, she held what appeared to be prescription eyeglasses.

To Schoonover, the description sounded like Diana Gaede, a.k.a. Diana Fruge. When Echevarria sat down with a sketch artist, though, the results weren't encouraging. On a scale of zero to ten, Echevarria gave the sketch only a 6.5 for accuracy. Pawlak then showed him a police booking photo of Fruge, taken when she was charged with shoplifting in 1985. She was 19 at the time. Echevarria couldn't say whether it was the same woman in her 30s who had dropped off the Cavalier.

Schoonover's gut told him it was.

An evidence technician in Hales Corners examined the car but found nothing useful. The experts at the Wisconsin state crime lab couldn't get to it for a couple of weeks.

Pawlak went back to the yellow pages. This time, his assignment was to call all the RV dealerships in the area, looking for a recent purchase by Tim Wicks, Dennis Gaede, Diana Gaede, Diana Fruge or any combination of the four names.

He struck pay dirt right away at Advance Camping Sales. They had sold a used RV to Fruge. In its former life, the vehicle had been used to transport a Boy Scout band. Fortunately for the authorities, it was anything but inconspicuous. There were Pabst Blue Ribbon beer decals on both doors, and large stickers announcing the occupants as the "Pioneer Drum and Bugle Corps." There was a dome light on the back that was supposed to flash, like the ones on highway maintenance vehicles, but it wasn't working.

Advance Camping Sales had more than a good description of the RV. They had a picture of it.

*   *   *

Schoonover called his colleagues together for a brainstorming session. Officer Lindenlaub, who had accompanied Schoonover to Wicks' apartment, vaguely recalled a bulletin about a John Doe found by the Michigan State Police a few weeks earlier. Like other notices from neighboring states, most of them irrelevant, the one from Michigan had been filed in a binder. Schoonover dug it out.

The announcement had been distributed to law enforcement agencies in 13 states. It described a headless, handless male body, age 40 to 50, 185 to 200 pounds, between 6'1" and 6'3", with a size 9 ¾ foot. The man had no tattoos, scars or other distinguishing characteristics.

The description sounded enough like Wicks for Schoonover to make a call to Michigan. He was connected to Sgt. Greg Tamlyn.

Schoonover was surprised to learn that the body was in the Milwaukee morgue. He was even more surprised when Tamlyn told him that the head, with a bullet in it, had recently been found on the Wisconsin side of the state line. The head, too, was in the Milwaukee morgue, Tamlyn said.

Schoonover called the medical examiner's office and was told they would need dental records to make the identification. There were hundreds of dentists in the Milwaukee area. How would he figure out which one was Wicks'?

Schoonover called Wicks' relatives and friends, but none knew the name of his dentist. Schoonover figured his last hope was, again, the phone book. His officers would

36

have to call the dentists from A to Z and ask if Wicks was a patient. Then Lindenlaub came to the rescue again. Lindenlaub told Schoonover he remembered a reminder card for a dentist's appointment stuck to Wicks' refrigerator.

Schoonover hoped it wasn't just wishful thinking on his colleague's part and headed back to the missing man's apartment. As soon as he walked in, Schoonover saw the reminder card on the refrigerator door.

Schoonover called the dentist's office and went to pick up the X-rays. The receptionist remembered Wicks as conscientious, friendly and trusting. She also remembered him being excited about a recent painting job at Marquette University. He'd never mentioned a Dennis or a band gig in Canada to her.

There was no telling how long it would take Milwaukee County's forensic dentist to look at the X-rays. Dr. L. Thomas Johnson, D.D.S. was an associate medical examiner, meaning he worked part time. Nonetheless, Schoonover wanted to drop off the films at the morgue right away so they would be available the next time Johnson came to the office. As Schoonover walked in the door, another man entered right behind him. That man happened to be Johnson.

Within two minutes, Johnson had made a positive identification. The skull in the morgue belonged to Wicks.

*   *   *

Beth and Tom Neary were packing for an upcoming move when Schoonover knocked on their door. Tom Neary expected a neighbor. Instead, he was greeted by Pawlak and Schoonover. Neary let them in, and the four of them sat on the couch, surrounded by boxes.

Schoonover showed the Nearys Gaede's mug shot and asked if they recognized him. They didn't.

"I'm afraid your brother is no longer with us," Schoonover said then.

"What do you mean, 'no longer with us'?" Neary asked.

"He's dead."

"And this son of a bitch did it, right?" Neary asked, pointing to the photo.

"We don't know for sure," Schoonover replied.

Neary asked about going to the morgue to identify the body, but Schoonover advised against it. "You want to remember him the way he was," the detective said.

After Schoonover said the word "dismembered," Neary imagined his brother-in-law chopped up in tiny pieces. He tried to keep that fact from his daughters, Samantha and Madeline, then 12 and 8, but Sam saw the details on the news. And the family couldn't ignore the crowd of reporters that would soon congregate outside their door.

Beth Neary sat in shock as her husband called her parents to tell them their son was dead.

Neary used the detective's euphemism.

"Tim's gone," he said to Wicks' mother.

"What do you mean, 'gone'?" she asked.

"He's dead."

Fay Wicks asked through her tears, "What happened?" But no one could give her an answer.

*   *   *

The same day, January 23, 2002, the Fargo Police pulled up outside the blue farmhouse in Gardner, North Dakota. They knew nobody was there. The man they thought was Wicks, and now knew was Gaede, hadn't shown his face at Compressed Air Technologies since the day Paridon snapped the Polaroid. The driveway was empty. Mail was piling up. The woman who worked at the post office across the street had been keeping an eye on things. She hadn't seen anyone.

38

The police decided they didn't need a full SWAT team with guns drawn to enter an empty house. Detectives Paul Lies and Chuck Sullivan would go inside to do an initial sweep, take photographs and look for obvious signs of trouble. Once they gave the all-clear, the other investigators could follow and begin to search for evidence of either an embezzlement from Compressed Air or the whereabouts of the real Tim Wicks, or both.

The Gardner farmhouse was technically outside the jurisdiction of the Fargo Police Department, since it was outside the city limits. Usually, with a crime in Fargo and evidence elsewhere in the county, a Cass County Sheriff's deputy would assist at the scene. That day the county's chief investigator, Lt. Rick Majerus, was in a staff meeting. Officers from the state's Bureau of Criminal Investigation would assist instead, and promised to page Majerus if they encountered problems.

Tammy Lynk sat in her car outside the house, waiting for the entry team to emerge. That's when her cell phone rang. It was her husband, but it wasn't a social call. Steve Lynk also worked for the Fargo Police Department. When Schoonover called in with urgent news from Hales Corners and Tammy wasn't available, the switchboard operator had transferred his call to Steve.

The color drained from Tammy Lynk's face as her husband spoke. The other officer in the car with her asked, "What? What? Are you okay?"

Lynk ended the call, absorbing the information Schoonover had relayed. A torso and a head had been identified using dental records. Tim Wicks was dead.

The entry team came out of the house, signaling the all-clear. Lynk jumped out of her car. "Time out!" she called. "We're dealing with a murder scene."

The group reassembled at the firehouse down the street where Lynk briefed the others on the details she knew. Things had changed dramatically. Lynk relinquished control of the investigation to the Cass County Sheriff's

Department. An officer was sent to the prosecutor's office to get State's Attorney Birch Burdick into the loop as soon as possible. They would have to re-write the warrant. They were no longer looking for just evidence of embezzlement. They were out to solve a murder.

The affidavit attached to the new warrant detailed what authorities in three states knew about Dennis Gaede and his relationship to Tim Wicks. It included all the evidence that Gaede had been living in Gardner, using Wicks' name. Then it described the discovery of Wicks' head and torso at the Menominee River.

By around 7 p.m., the new warrant was signed. Investigators donned protective suits, booties and caps before entering the home to avoid contaminating any evidence that might be there. They also wore gloves.

Some of the most promising evidence led investigators to believe someone had cleaned up a bloody mess: a mop head with a brownish stain on it, spots that looked like blood near the washer and dryer, a smear near the banister. There were boxes of several types of ammunition and a couple of holsters, but no guns. Also telling was a receipt from Palladin Enterprises for a kit called, "Relocating under a new identity/modern identity."

Lies, Sullivan, Lynk and the others took samples of the stains. They collected hairs and carpet fibers. They even cut out squares of linoleum. Once they had finished collecting evidence, investigators sprayed the whole place with Luminol, a chemical used to detect the presence of blood. Even if blood has been thoroughly cleaned up, residual components react with Luminol, causing a surface to glow.

Lies had been a crime scene investigator for more than a dozen years, but he had never seen Luminol do what it did in the kitchen of the Gardner house. When he sprayed the floor, it lit up like a Christmas tree. Not just one spot or splatter, but the whole floor, like it had once been covered with buckets of blood.

Outside, Lies walked around the property looking for clues. He paused beside the barn that Gaede and his family had been using as a garage. On the north side of the building, in a grassy area not quite covered with snow, there were dig marks. Lies could picture a backhoe, its teeth penetrating just a couple of inches into the frozen ground.

Officers pawed through trash bags in the basement and combed the lot next door, finding nothing useful. Lies even sprayed the trash bags with Luminol for good measure, to no avail. The boxes in the garage held bobbers and other fishing accessories.

Lynk and her colleagues spent hours on their hands and knees, digging through the snow and frozen dirt of the back yard, but there was nothing more. They gazed into a cistern on the property, thinking it would be a perfect hiding place. One detective tied a rope around his waist, and the others lowered him down. He shone a flashlight on the ice below, hoping for a glimpse of something. Anything. A gun. The clothing Wicks was wearing when he died. His drums. His hands.

There was nothing.

Majerus, who would later take over as lead investigator on the case, showed up on the scene around 10:30 p.m.

"It was kind of funny," Majerus recalled. "He's here, but he's dead, and we're doing a search warrant at his house. That's when it all became clear as mud."

In his nearly 30 years with the sheriff's department, Majerus had worked to solve about a dozen murders. Many of them were strange, like the Paulie Johnson case. The daughter of a state highway patrolman, she was shot and killed after surprising a burglar in her family's house. All the while, her dad's marked squad car was parked outside in the yard.

The Wicks case wasn't the first dismemberment Majerus had seen, either. Back in 1978, the body of 21-

41

year-old Billy Wolf was found in two garbage bags in the Red River. It had been chopped in half at the waist.

Majerus hoped the case at hand would turn out better than the Wolf case. Three months after Wolf's body was found, his father was charged with the killing. Prosecutors soon dropped the charges for lack of evidence. About 10 years later, authorities re-opened the case and decided it was drug-related. They tracked down some suspects and were pretty sure they had determined the scene of the crime, but never came up with enough proof to issue charges.

The search of the Gardner property didn't end until 3:30 a.m. Authorities walked away with a list of evidence long enough to fill three pages. But they couldn't be sure if they were at the scene of a homicide.

Shortly after Schoonover called Steve Lynk with the news of a homicide, he called Tamlyn and told him to close the book on the case of the unidentified body from the Nathan Bridge. Schoonover told Tamlyn they had recovered Wicks' car, but they had no evidence from it yet, because there was a backlog at the State Crime Lab. Tamlyn had good news. Michigan could take Wicks' car for immediate processing, he said. He promised to send a flatbed truck to pick it up.

Neither Gaede's name nor Wicks' rang a bell with the Michigan sergeant. Then Tamlyn did some checking and discovered that Dennis Gaede and a woman named Lorelie Gaede owned property in northern Menominee County, about 17 miles from the point where the body was dumped and 21 miles from where the surveyor found the head.

Neighbors recalled seeing a U-Haul-type truck outside the house around the time the body was found.

Using information from both Wisconsin and North Dakota, Tamlyn applied for his own search warrant. The Gaede property could best be described as a camp, and the house on it was a shack. The dilapidated building's outer walls were multi-colored brick on the bottom, siding on the top. There was no plumbing. At the time Tamlyn and his team conducted their search, plastic had been taped over the windows to block out the wind.

Tamlyn was optimistic as he wrote his affidavit. In the DNA age, it didn't take much. He felt sure his team would find some useful evidence, even if they couldn't prove a homicide. If Wicks' DNA was in Gaede's house, they could at least charge him with dismembering a corpse, a 10-year felony.

A judge signed the warrant and the Michigan State Police spent almost four hours searching the Gaede property. Almost immediately it was clear nothing nefarious had happened in that house. There was no sign that Wicks had been killed or dismembered there. There were few tools, no weapons, no trash bags. The furniture wasn't dusty, but the place appeared abandoned.

The team recovered a small hand saw with a wooden handle and several pieces of rope. Hair and possible blood samples were collected, but none yielded enough DNA for analysis. It was another dead end.

As the authorities searched in North Dakota and Michigan, Gaede, Fruge and her young son, Joshua, showed up at Fruge's ex-husband's house in Wisconsin so Joshua could visit with his half-sister, Raychel, Fruge's teen-age daughter from her first marriage. No one told the police about the visit until days after the fact. By then, the three had disappeared.

CHAPTER SIX

When Detective Devan Gracyalny heard about the case of the missing man from Hales Corners, it sounded strangely familiar. Gracyalny worked in West Allis, a Milwaukee suburb not far from Hales Corners. West Allis was also the place Gaede and Fruge called home before they fled to North Dakota.

Just two months before Wicks disappeared, Gracyalny had investigated Gaede in connection with another strange case. Robert Tobiason was found dead in a motel room in Albuquerque, New Mexico on October 5, 2001. The police questioned how he got there, since he didn't have a car. Tobiason had lived in the same building as Gaede and Fruge, and the key to their apartment was found in the motel room with his body.

The body was found in a bathtub, the water still running. The door was unlocked, but the chain was on, requiring the police to kick it in. There was only one small window in the room, too small for Gaede to fit through.

Tobiason, known around his Wisconsin neighborhood as "Mr. Bob," suffered from both mental illness and Parkinson's disease. Although Gracyalny had found the presence of Gaede's key odd, everything else pointed to natural causes.

When Gracyalny heard about the Wicks case, he became less certain. He called Hales Corners and spoke to Officer Gary Lindenlaub, who had been assisting Schoonover in the investigation. Gracyalny promised to call the medical examiner who had looked at Tobiason's body, just to be sure. He also planned to ask a few questions about who had prepared Tobiason's tax forms the year before.

For Schoonover, the news about Tobiason was distressing. Was it just a coincidence that two of Gaede's acquaintances had turned up dead, or was something more sinister at work? Schoonover was determined to find Dennis Gaede and interrogate him.

After a few simple background checks, Gaede's motive for assuming Wicks' identity became clear: He was a wanted man with a criminal past in both the United States and Canada.

The Hales Corners Police Department couldn't spare the time or the money to send Schoonover to Canada without a concrete lead. They couldn't easily do without their sole detective for a trip to Gaede's former homes in the far reaches of Wisconsin, either, as long as they weren't sure of jurisdiction. So Schoonover located people in the Milwaukee area with ties to Gaede. Among the first ones he found was the co-owner of the Michigan property, Gaede's ex-wife, Lorelie.

Gaede and Lorelie divorced in 1995. Years later, Lorelie would say things fell apart when their two kids accused him of sexual abuse. Gaede denied it, and charges were never filed. In their divorce papers, Lorelie cited Gaede's mental abuse of her as the only reason the marriage was irreparably broken.

By the time Schoonover came knocking on her door, her son was 16; her daughter was 18. Their father owed approximately $45,000 in back child support. "If I'd known then what I know now, I never would have married him," Lorelie told Schoonover. Gaede, she said, owned a towing company during most of their marriage. But what he really did was scam people.

"Do you know anything about Lodis Financial Group?" Schoonover asked, wondering about the tax business that became Wicks' downfall.

"No," she answered.

"There's a cross-reference to you when I ran a check on the company," Schoonover informed her.

It seemed to make sense to Gaede's ex-wife. She had been wondering why all kinds of creditors were calling her to talk about some business Gaede had.

Schoonover asked if Gaede was a trained accountant or CPA.

"No," Lorelie answered. She told the detective Gaede was very intelligent but had no formal training in any field.

Lorelie, who worked at a Wal-Mart near her home in Germantown, another Milwaukee suburb, had just one remaining tie to Gaede. She would soon be the owner of his family's cabin in Powers, Michigan, the one Tamlyn had already searched for evidence.

The Michigan cabin didn't have indoor plumbing — there was an outhouse — and was often full of bugs, Lorelie told Schoonover. Although it was primitive, the cabin remained the source of an ongoing family dispute, and not just between Gaede and his ex-wife. It had belonged to Gaede's mother, Hazel, and many family members enjoyed going up there on the weekends. At some point Hazel had signed the property over to Gaede, and he decided he didn't want anyone else using the place. He changed the locks. His sisters, in turn, broke in and changed the locks again. Now it seemed no one ever had a working key for the place.

As part of the divorce, Gaede was ordered to either sell the shack and its acre of land (worth about $8,800 at the time) and give Lorelie half the proceeds, or buy out her half. He had done neither.

When Gaede didn't pay the cabin's property taxes, she got the opportunity to become the full owner. If she paid the taxes for seven years, the property would be hers, free and clear. Lorelie had been paying the tax bills for five years by the time Schoonover came to see her in early 2002.

Lorelie suggested that Schoonover speak with Gaede's niece, Tanya Gonzalez. Schoonover decided the suggestion was a good one and went to find Gonzalez, whose mother, Kathy Alm, was Gaede's sister. Gonzalez told Schoonover that although Gaede legally owned the

Michigan cabin, his sisters were the ones who maintained it.

Around the time Wicks' body was found, some things were out of place, Gonzalez told Schoonover. A hand saw wasn't where it belonged, and an ax they didn't recognize had appeared. When Gonzalez's mother lifted the steel cover over an abandoned well on the property, she found evidence that something had been burned inside. No one called to report a break-in. They just assumed Gaede had been there again.

Gonzalez gave Schoonover a list of Gaede's relatives up in Michigan. Several of them owned land for hunting, she said, and she suspected Gaede might be hiding out in the woods up there.

After his chat with Gonzalez, Schoonover tracked Hazel Gaede, Dennis' mother, through her car's license plates. When he arrived at her house, no one was there. A neighbor told Schoonover Hazel worked at a nearby Laundromat, where her shift usually ended at 10:30 p.m. Hazel Gaede was decidedly unhelpful.

"When did you last see your son, Dennis?" Schoonover asked after introducing himself.

"A long time ago," she answered.

"What does that mean?" Schoonover prompted.

"A while," she said with a shrug.

Schoonover suspected Hazel was lying, and he sensed he wasn't going to get any cooperation from her. He gave her his business card and asked her to call if she saw Gaede, although he knew she would not.

Meanwhile, tips poured in from Wicks' friends. Susanna Stevens, who had known Wicks 23 years, said she had last seen him in the early morning hours of December 28. Wicks was a regular at a bar in the blue-collar suburb of Cudahy called Vic's Clique, and often showed up at the Thursday night jam sessions she organized there, Stevens said. When she last saw him three days after Christmas,

Wicks was with a man named either Dennis or Dan, Stevens told Schoonover. She hadn't seen him since.

Schoonover showed Stevens a photo array, but she couldn't pick out Gaede. Then Schoonover showed Stevens another photo, which pictured Gaede with two women. Stevens said she didn't recognize any of them.

Meanwhile, Gracyalny got in touch with the medical examiner in Albuquerque, who told him, unequivocally, that Tobiason had died of natural causes. The key in his motel room, it seemed, was a red herring.

*　　　　　　*　　　　　　*

Jim Koehler found out Wicks was dead by watching the television news. It was a 10 p.m. newscast sometime near the end of January. The gruesome details about a decapitated body and its missing head being identified caught Koehler's attention. Then he heard Wicks' name and saw his picture on the screen. Koehler couldn't believe it.

Koehler had called Wicks' apartment a couple of times. He figured it would take a month or two, max, for Wicks to come back, shrugging his shoulders as he sheepishly talked about the Canada gig that didn't pan out.

Wicks would cope with the disappointment fine, Koehler predicted. Wicks had a lot going for him before he left for Canada, including $17,000 he'd inherited from his aunt.

"I should really buy a house, shouldn't I?" Wicks had asked in one of his more practical moods.

Koehler had agreed that would be a good idea. After a lot of discussion, Wicks decided a condo might be a better idea. He started filling out the papers to apply for a mortgage. One of the credit reports showed some strange activity on his credit cards. He'd been confused, but not overly concerned.

Now Wicks would never get his condo.

It didn't take long for Koehler, Sauter and Wicks' other friends to decide that the place to honor him was Vic's Clique. The memorial jam night took place on February 8, 2002. Wicks' buddies from the music scene drank beer, played Wicks' favorite songs and shared memories of their friend.

One summer, Sauter recalled, Wicks organized a group of guys to make the 80-mile trip from Milwaukee to Chicago for the legendary Blues Fest. The motley group took the train south and spent an afternoon drinking beer and drinking in the sights and sounds. Then Wicks suddenly remembered he had shopping to do. He'd heard about a sale at Marshall Field's department store. He assured his friends the store was nearby, and the walk would be worth their while.

After walking several miles from the Grant Park Blues Fest, Wicks' buddies were exhausted, sweaty and not in good spirits upon their arrival. Wicks led them through the men's department, failing to find the obscure sale on t-shirts he'd heard about from some random audience member at the festival. Finally, just as Sauter had reached the end of his rope, Wicks found the rumored t-shirts in a pile in the basement of the 10-story store. The shirts came in solid colors, with little decoration. Plain old t-shirts, the kind you could get almost anywhere back in Milwaukee. They were selling for $5 each. Wicks bought several, convinced the bargain had been worth their two-hour detour. Sauter wasn't so sure. Yet Wicks' excitement over his simple purchase made it impossible for his friends to stay angry.

As the stories and songs flowed through the memorial jam, Wicks' friends took up a collection for the Wisconsin Conservatory of Music, where Wicks and Sauter met in 1992 and where Wicks often hung out and helped the teachers. Sauter got the feeling Wicks stayed around the school because he didn't like to leave the music.

By the end of the semester, the two had formed a blues combo with Sauter on keyboard and Wicks on drums. They played minor gigs in Milwaukee clubs, including a dive called the Up and Under Pub and the VFW Post near Milwaukee's Mitchell International Airport.

Every now and then, a particularly good-looking lady would catch Wicks' eye. "Hang a left," he would call out. "She went that way." Although he rarely smoked, Wicks would often chase the women down and ask for a cigarette as a way to start up a conversation.

Although Schoonover wasn't officially on duty the night of Wicks' barroom memorial, the detective attended. As he stood in the smoky bar among Wicks' eclectic group of friends, Schoonover realized Wicks' killer had underestimated them. With no wife, no children, no roommate, no regular job and no daily or even weekly communication with his relatives, the killer probably thought no one would miss Wicks. The killer hadn't counted on the dedication of Wicks' starving-artist friends, who would raise $776 in his memory that night. The killer hadn't counted on the persistence of Bruce Sauter, whose nagging had driven Schoonover to action.

Even so, Schoonover thought, the killer had come close to committing the perfect crime. If not for a series of strange coincidences, Wicks' body would never have been identified, and his friends and loved ones would have been left to wonder.

As the investigation progressed, Schoonover shrugged off compliments about his brilliant detective work, both in identifying the body and in pinpointing a suspect. "It was just good luck," he would say.

The ones who really deserved credit, in Schoonover's opinion, were the members of Wicks' family. For them, the recovery and identification of the body were just the beginning of a long ordeal.

Wicks' family remained remarkably patient. For 11 months, they weren't allowed to claim his body. No coroner wanted to issue a death certificate, since one county was responsible for the head and another had jurisdiction over the torso. The Milwaukee authorities, who still had the remains in their morgue, were convinced the crime had occurred outside their jurisdiction. They feared a signed death certificate in Wisconsin could help the killer in court wherever he ended up.

Without his body, Wicks' family couldn't file any insurance claims or empty his apartment. Yet unlike many victims' families Schoonover had dealt with over the course of his career, they didn't complain. They didn't nag, and they didn't yell. They just trusted the Hales Corners detective and hoped for closure.

Schoonover didn't want to let them down, but he felt powerless to help them. The murder had most likely occurred in North Dakota's Cass County, where the Gardner farmhouse was located. Schoonover thought if the prosecutor there would sign off on it, the Milwaukee medical examiner would release the body. Schoonover made call after call to State's Attorney Birch Burdick in Fargo. At first, Burdick was uncooperative. Then he stopped taking Schoonover's calls.

In the end, after much cajoling by Schoonover alone, the Milwaukee County Medical Examiner agreed that Wicks could be laid to rest just before Thanksgiving 2002. Wicks' family never had a funeral or a memorial service. When the medical examiner finally released his body, it was cremated, and the remains were buried in the family plot in Ashland. For Wicks' family, the burial provided some consolation. Still, they were haunted by what had happened to him. Even more troubling was the thought that his killer might never be brought to justice.

CHAPTER SEVEN

Schoonover thought about the Wicks case often. Again and again, he came back to the thought that the man didn't have to die. Homicide was always a terrible thing. For Schoonover, knowing the victim was so harmless, so innocent, just made it worse.

A mental image of the victim emerged more clearly as time went by. Schoonover pictured Wicks as a laid-back, easygoing guy. Very personable. Maybe too nice for his own good. Maybe a bit naïve. His relatives had creative metaphors to describe how giving he was. If he was lying on the battlefield, bleeding, his brother-in-law once said, he'd ask you if you needed blood.

The more Schoonover learned about Wicks, the more determined the detective became to bring the drummer's killer to justice.

Wicks' father, John Wicks, a part-time radio announcer, met Fay Uline when the two were students at Northland College, a liberal arts school in their hometown of Ashland, Wisconsin. The two were married in 1952 and moved to a Cape Cod-style home on a wooded lot in Wauwatosa, a western suburb of Milwaukee. Their son, Timothy Walker Wicks, was a honeymoon baby. Daughter Beth followed four years later. The children often spent summers at their grandparents' cottage on the bluffs of Lake Superior. There, they swam, fished, went boating and practiced water skiing.

During those summers, Tim Wicks became a strong enough swimmer to earn a spot on the swim team at Wauwatosa West High School — and to save his little sister's life.

"I got in a little too deep," Beth recalled. "The waves got a little too high. The water was coming over my head."

Her big brother jumped into the lake and pulled Beth out.

Even more than swimming, Tim Wicks loved the drums. As far back as elementary school, he played the snare drum. When he practiced, the souvenir plates his mother had hung on the walls of their tidy little home would vibrate, and she would leave.

Wicks was a good student when he wanted to apply himself, which wasn't often. Beth recalls their mother repeatedly yelling at her brother to finish his school work and to show a little school spirit. Wicks earned his best grades in math, especially algebra. When playing darts with four or five friends, he could add all the scores in his head.

Beth recalls her brother drinking a lot, then coming home at 3 a.m. to make frozen pizza. When he left for college, her parents weren't sorry to see him go.

At Beth's wedding, Wicks wasn't content to be the brother of the bride. He kicked the drummer of the band she had hired off the stage. "Okay, what are we playing?" he asked the stunned remnants of the band. Then he played along with any song they chose. In Tom Neary's opinion, that was Wicks' greatest musical strength. He could play anything, in any style, and didn't have the super ego that prevented so many musicians from taking instruction.

Neary shared Wicks' love of music. At family gatherings, the two sometimes jammed together, or Neary played Wicks the songs he had written. Neary often thought his brother-in-law would make a fine studio musician, backing up recording artists as Neary himself had once done. Neary even suggested such a career path to Wicks several times.

"You're right," Wicks would say. But he never followed through.

Wicks spent just one semester at Berklee, the exclusive music school in Boston. Beth doesn't know what went wrong. She wrote to him a couple of times while he was there, but he never wrote back. After dropping out of

54

school, Wicks bummed around Boston for a couple of years, drumming in the evenings, doing odd jobs and living the carefree bachelor's life. When he came back, he was different.

In high school, Wicks drank a lot and smoked some pot. His family suspected he'd experimented with something stronger in Boston. It was like he was Peter Pan, stuck forever in the Neverland of the teen years. "Tim, the drugs wrecked your brain," his mother would say. Wicks would apologize but not elaborate.

"I truly believe that if he hadn't taken those drugs and he was more in touch with reality, this would never have happened," Neary said of his brother-in-law's death. "Tim wasn't stupid. By no means was he an idiot. He was just out there trying to survive."

Despite their dedication to the Episcopal church, John and Fay Wicks never shoved religion down their children's throats. When the teen-age Tim resisted attending services, his parents didn't force the issue. He converted to Catholicism about six months before he disappeared and embraced his new religion with zeal, handing out pamphlets and preaching the occasional barroom sermon.

Even with his newfound faith, his mother agreed that Tim was better off as a bachelor. "Heaven forbid he meets someone like him and they have kids," she would say. Wicks realized he wasn't equipped for the responsibility of having children of his own. Yet he admirably filled the role of uncle to Beth and Tom's two daughters. Beth recalls him sitting on the couch between Sam and Madeline, reading books for hours. At Christmas and on their birthdays, the girls expected to be spoiled by their Uncle Tim, and he obliged.

Wicks was arrested just once, in 1999. He and Neary had a few too many drinks at a family dinner in a restaurant. Neary complained that Wicks was being too loud and offending the little old ladies at the next table with his profane language. "I pushed him out the door," Neary recalled. "He clocked me. I clocked him, and someone called the police." Both men were taken to jail, but no charges were filed. It was the most embarrassing incident of his life, Neary says, and the two were able to laugh about it later.

The story about the fight seemed typical of Wicks' reaction to trouble. The Tim Wicks that Schoonover learned about didn't seem to hold a grudge and wasn't vindictive in any way. Schoonover could imagine Wicks finding out Gaede had stolen his identity and telling his friend, "Don't worry about it, man." Wicks probably wouldn't even have called the police.

With the permission of Wicks' parents, Schoonover started collecting the dead man's mail. The detective sorted through bills, coupons and credit card offers, carefully examining anything that looked remotely personal. The December 2001 bill for Wicks' Visa card piqued Schoonover's interest. Perhaps it contained clues about what had happened in the last days of the drummer's life. Schoonover discovered a virtual line of demarcation in the middle of the statement. Before Christmas, there were the expected purchases at malls and big box stores near Wicks' Hales Corners home. Shortly thereafter, however, the Visa card made its way to North Dakota, then Michigan. That's when things got really interesting.

On Saturday, December 29, the card was used at United Rentals in Fargo to rent a small backhoe and a trailer. The total cost for both was $286.46. Schoonover learned that the rental agency was closed on Sundays. When it opened again the following Monday morning, the equipment was back in the parking lot.

On December 30, the credit card was used at Mills Fleet Farm, one of a chain of stores with locations in North Dakota, Wisconsin, Minnesota and Iowa that offers supplies for camping, hunting, fishing and yard work. Wicks' credit card was used to purchase $200.30 worth of items. Even before Schoonover saw the surveillance tapes, he suspected Wicks hadn't bought home improvement supplies. The list of purchases included burlap bags, twine, a hatchet, a tree pruner, a hand saw, a box of 45-gallon trash bags, an extension cord and mini lamp, several pairs of gloves, and men's camouflage hunting boots — size 13. Schoonover had not forgotten the original bulletin that the Michigan State Police sent out when Wicks' body was found. His feet were size 9 ¾, not 13.

The items from Fleet Farm, it seemed to Schoonover, were an amateur body disposal kit. He didn't waste any time obtaining the store's surveillance video. On it, Gaede strolled carelessly into the store. Fruge and Joshua were a few paces behind as she laughed with a store employee near the door. Gaede meandered through the aisles, selecting the items Schoonover later saw listed on the receipt. His family rejoined him near the register.

As Schoonover watched the video, he realized Gaede had never expected Wicks' body to be identified. With no body, no one would have a reason to examine the credit card receipts or look at the security video. The people in the stores would continue to think they were dealing with Tim Wicks, just as everyone else in Fargo had.

But now that the police knew Wicks was dead, the credit card gave Schoonover a tactical advantage. He could use it to track Gaede's movements. And Gaede was definitely on the move. At 2:18 p.m. on New Year's Day 2002, the card was used to purchase more than 20 gallons of diesel fuel at a Citgo gas station and convenience store in Iron Mountain, Michigan, not far from Gaede's cabin in Powers.

The Citgo, like the Fleet Farm, had an extensive surveillance system. The man in the grainy photo was large and balding, with glasses. It was impossible to make a positive identification, but Schoonover knew he was once again looking at Gaede.

By January 4, the Visa card had made its way back to Fargo, where it was used to pay for the rental of a U-Haul truck from the facility on Main Avenue downtown.

Fargo Detective Paul Lies and Special Agent John Dalziel of the FBI paid a visit and talked with the U-Haul manager, Kevin Liedhal. Wicks' card was first used on December 30 to rent a 14-foot diesel truck and to purchase a padlock, tape, a tape dispenser, five furniture pads and four wardrobe boxes, according to Liedhal's records.

"Could a person fit a body in there?" Liedhal was asked later.

"Yeah, you could."

"How would a person fit a body in there?"

"Pretty much just put it together and drop 'em in," Liedhal replied. "You could always put two together. They telescope together pretty easy."

That first swipe of the Visa card didn't show up on Wicks' bill because Liedhal didn't put the charges through until the U-Haul truck was returned four days later. At that time, Liedhal said, the odometer showed 1,786 miles driven during what was supposed to be a local move.

The police asked to see one of the furniture pads. Liedhal didn't have the specific ones purchased with the card because those hadn't been returned, but he gave the officers one that he said was similar. It was more like a blanket for a queen-size bed. Like the fibers found on Wicks' body, it was blue.

Lies and Dalziel sent the blanket to Milwaukee to be compared with the fibers found on Wicks' body. Even if they proved to be similar, such blankets were used in moving trucks of every variety every day. It would be just another piece of the circumstantial evidence. But the fibers didn't match.

Worse, by the time Lies and Dalziel interviewed Liedhal, the U-Haul truck in question had already been rented by someone else and wasn't on the lot for them to examine. The manager didn't recall anything strange about the truck's condition when the man calling himself Wicks brought it back. Certainly there was no blood in back — nothing to indicate a dismembered corpse had been there.

The aluminum floor of the truck's cargo space looked perfectly normal, Liedhal said.

The truck was scheduled to be returned later that evening and already had been reserved for rent the following day. Lies and Dalziel instructed Liedhal to call when the vehicle was returned and told him not to rent it again until the police could examine it.

It seemed another promising lead had slipped away. Even if there was trace evidence in the U-Haul, it would be almost useless. Any defense attorney in town could argue that anything collected from the truck was tainted as a result of the fact that it had been cleaned and re-rented. Even so, the truck was later taken to the Fargo Police Department's evidence shed to await examination by the FBI's evidence response team.

Before anyone could get too discouraged, Schoonover found another lead in the stack of mail. It was a statement from Marshall and Ilsley Bank, known around Wisconsin as M&I Bank, where Wicks had a savings account. There were several withdrawals listed in mid-January. Schoonover knew it was impossible Wicks had done any banking then. He was already dead.

Again, Schoonover reviewed surveillance video. On December 21 and December 26, the video showed a man withdrawing money from Tim Wicks' account. Schoonover recognized the man as the real Tim Wicks. But on New Year's Day 2002, Dennis Gaede withdrew $1,500.

Less than two weeks later, on January 10, a man called about closing out a certificate of deposit valued at nearly $14,000 that Wicks held at the bank. Via telephone, the money could only be transferred to another account for later withdrawal, the customer service representative told the caller. The bank could mail a check. Otherwise, the customer would have to come in to one of the branches. The caller said he wanted the money transferred. He gave the correct account numbers for both Wicks' CD and his savings account and, for security purposes, Wicks' mother's maiden name of Uline.

A day later, Gaede showed up to make a withdrawal. The teller, Ann Furey, remembered the encounter vividly and described it to Schoonover in detail.

The man approached the teller window with the withdrawal slip already filled out.

"Do you want this in a check?" she asked.

"No," the man answered. "I need cash." Then, by way of explanation, he added, "I'm buying an RV, and the guy I'm buying it from wants cash."

"I could give you a cashier's check," Furey suggested. "It's really not safe to walk around with that much cash."

"That's okay. I still want the cash," he said.

Furey told him there was government paperwork she would need to complete that was required for large cash transactions. Gaede told her he was a self-employed accountant and he knew all about those forms. Furey stuffed the money into two envelopes and gave it to the man. He walked calmly out of the bank.

Six days later, a man who looked like Gaede approached the drive-up window of a different M&I branch. He was driving Wicks' Cavalier. He withdrew $500 from the savings account, leaving $272.02 behind. The teller asked for identification and wrote a North Dakota driver's license number on the withdrawal slip. The number matched a license issued to Tim Wicks, but the picture matched none other than Dennis Gaede.

After that, the trail went cold. By mid-February, there was still no sign of Gaede. Desperate to find him, authorities turned to the media. At a Fargo press conference, Lt. Rick Majerus of the Cass County Sheriff's Department and FBI Special Agent Ray Morrow described Gaede as a federal fugitive and warned the public that he was dangerous. Hoping for press coverage in North Dakota, South Dakota, Minnesota, Wisconsin and Michigan, they passed out photos of Gaede, Fruge, Joshua and the RV. They asked anyone with information to call the Cass County Sheriff's Department or their local police. Then they waited for the phone to ring.

*   *   *

The recreational vehicle lifestyle attracts all sorts of people, from retirees to snowbirds to "workampers," who take jobs at campgrounds around the country in exchange for a free place to stay. RV parks become temporary communities in which people share campfires, play sports and generally get to know each other. Sometimes they keep in touch, meeting up again down the road. Living in an RV is a good way to get away from the cold or to see the country. Or, Gaede and Fruge thought, to stay a step ahead of the law.

A man who would later use the alias Duane Strute and his wife often left their home in Crookston, Minnesota, just across the state line from Fargo, to camp in warmer climates during the brutal northern winters. In January and February 2002, they spent several days at the Two Rivers Campground, an RV park outside Nashville, Tennessee.

One day in the campground's laundry room, Strute's wife had an encounter with the woman whose family had parked their RV next to the Strutes'. The stranger, who was drinking a beer as she folded clothes, seemed friendly at first, and she was chatty. The woman told Mrs. Strute that she, her husband and their son were from Gardner, North Dakota, and started living in their RV after they became homeless. Her husband, the woman said, was a drummer who hoped to join a band in Nashville. The woman held up a shirt. "My husband weighs 250 pounds," she told Mrs. Strute. "See how big they are? It takes forever to dry."

Mrs. Strute listened politely and smiled at the woman's little boy. She thought him to be about kindergarten age. The boy began to introduce himself, but before he could finish, his mother clapped her hand over his mouth. "Shush," she told him. "I don't think they want to know your name." Then she sent him off to get her another beer.

Mrs. Strute, feeling uneasy, went back to her camper.

"There's something funny with those people," she told her husband. "I think they kidnapped that child." Her husband told her not to be ridiculous.

The last night they stayed at the Tennessee campground, Mrs. Strute's husband went out for a while. The 250-pound man whose wife had washed his shirts in the laundry room just sat in a chair in his camper, staring in the direction of the Strutes' camper, for hours. Mrs. Strute couldn't sleep. She closed the curtains and turned off all the lights.

At 4 a.m., Mrs. Strute looked out again. The man was still there, still looking right in her direction.

CHAPTER EIGHT

East Troy, Wisconsin, is one of Milwaukee's bedroom communities. Its residents travel Interstate Highway 43 northeast downtown, where they work, eat dinner and socialize. Back in the '80s, when Diana Fruge was growing up, about 3,000 people called East Troy home, and most knew one another.

Every now and then, someone in East Troy died of unnatural causes. Most of the time the homicides were domestic or the result of family squabbles. Property crimes were more common. As local farmers sold their acreage to real estate developers and the community expanded, the cops got busier with burglaries. Still, the petty crimes were fairly easy to solve. All an enterprising cop had to do was find a teenager with an appearance in traffic court looming and offer to fix the ticket. In time, the teen made sure the grapevine went to work and revealed the culprit. Inevitably, the guilty kid's clueless parents would frown in disbelief and say something like, "But I moved out here to get *away* from crime."

The whole town got together every Fourth of July at what the locals called the "ETBT," the East Troy Beer Tent. The tent was part of a traveling festival, complete with carnival games, makeshift bars and music. It visited several small towns across Wisconsin every summer. In most towns, the tent stayed for a day or two before moving to its next destination. East Troy was the only town that claimed the tent for five days. The Lions Club raffled off a Harley Davidson motorcycle — manufactured in Milwaukee, about 40 miles away — and always made a ton of money on the tickets.

Diana Fruge's parents ran a convenience store with an extensive liquor department called the Trading Post. It stood across the street from the police station, and cops getting off their shifts were regular customers.

Fruge's class at East Troy High School had fewer than 200 students. She describes her childhood as happy, although she admits spending her teen years waging a battle for acceptance. At 14, she had her stomach stapled to combat a weight problem that had plagued her all her life. Nevertheless, Fruge, born Diana Wutke, weighed close to 200 pounds throughout most of her high school days and had a hard time finding boys who were interested in her. High school was also the place she discovered one of the unfortunate side effects of bariatric surgery: her newly designed stomach absorbed alcohol faster.

For the most part, life was good for Fruge, her two sisters and her brother — until her parents divorced. A small town loves a good scandal, and Fruge's father provided one. He left her mother for a younger woman who, in turn, left her husband.

Fruge, whom nearly everyone called Diane, was 19 at the time. She had been working as a bartender since graduating from high school the year before, in 1984, and felt fortunate that she had a portable career. When the East Troy rumor mill became too much to bear, she headed for Florida. Within two years, one of her regular customers at the bar, Rayallen Fruge, progressed from boyfriend to husband. They were married by a justice of the peace in 1987. Later that year, their daughter, Raychel, was born.

The family moved back to Wisconsin so Raychel could be close to her aunts, uncle and grandmother. At 25, Fruge went to Milwaukee's Eric of Norway Beauty School, turning her natural obsession with hair and makeup into a career. She called her clients and practically everyone else "honey." Her husband repaired vehicles in an auto body shop.

Eventually, the young mother opened her own beauty salon. One of the stylists she hired was a short Hispanic man named Cayatano Barranco. Like everyone else, Fruge called him Brando. Eventually, she promoted him to salon manager. From the day they met, there was an unspoken attraction between the two. Although she tried to resist his macho charms, Fruge eventually gave in, cheating on the husband she considered a good and decent man. When she discovered she was pregnant with Barranco's child, Fruge told her husband everything. Then she took her daughter, moved in with her lover, and filed for divorce.

Eventually, she realized she had made a horrible mistake. Fruge was several months pregnant the day she went at Barranco with a knife. She was tired, so tired, of the yelling, the screaming, the hitting. She had to protect her baby. She just had to get out of there. Only Barranco wouldn't let her go, she later explained. That's why she grabbed the butcher knife from the block on the kitchen counter. She swung wildly, connecting with his fingers as she fled.

The destructive nature of the relationship finally sank in when their son, Joshua, was learning to talk. One day he snuggled into his mother's lap, looked at her adoringly, and said, "I love you, motherfucker." It took everything she had not to cry.

After that, Fruge left for good, but she would never be totally free of her five-and-a-half-year relationship with Barranco. They would always be Joshua's parents.

Fruge met Dennis Gaede a short time later, in early 2001. Gaede was the youngest of five children. He and his four older sisters, Sue, Barb, Kathy and Sharon, had three different fathers. More than 20 years separated the oldest from the youngest.

Sue often cared for her little brother, who was fairly spoiled. Often, Gaede was treated like an only child because he was by far the youngest and the only boy.

The family lived on Milwaukee's north side and attended Catholic Mass at Mother of Perpetual Help almost every Sunday. Gaede's father sold cars, while his mother worked as a visiting nurse and delivered newspapers. Young Gaede sometimes helped her with her route.

Gaede became interested in the drums at age 4, banging on pots and pans while listening to Beatles records. Later he learned to play the guitar, bass guitar, clarinet and cello. He formed his first band, Wild Hurricane, when he was 11. At Milwaukee's Custer High School, Gaede played the drums in the school band and had a spot on the football team. He was known to cause some mischief, once filling a girl's coat pockets with big, slimy worms during science class.

Gaede's father died in 1986 after a series of heart attacks and strokes. Gaede was 23. By the time Gaede met Fruge, he was 37. She was two years younger and worked 30 hours a week cutting hair, in addition to managing two apartment buildings. One of them was the West Allis building where she lived.

Gaede was renting office space below the apartments. He called his accounting business Lodis Financial Group, although he seemed to be the group's only member. He was busiest during tax season, as people answered an ad he had placed in the paper: tax preparation for $25. One of those clients was Timothy Wicks. Even after Wicks' tax forms were completed, he would drop by Gaede's office and chat from time to time. Fruge found Wicks kind of goofy and often obnoxious. She wasn't surprised that he had never married.

Gaede's second business enterprise was Hudson Bay Bait and Tackle, where he sold live bait and a complete line of fishing equipment. It was open seven days a week, and Gaede kept a small pistol behind the register for protection.

Fruge initially thought of Gaede as the friendly guy who worked downstairs, nothing more. She'd never pictured herself with a guy who looked like him. He weighed more than 250 pounds, wore glasses, and didn't have much hair. But he was sweet, enthusiastic and funny.

After a few weeks, Gaede started dropping by Fruge's place for a beer after work. Sometimes, he'd bring food for Fruge and the kids. She would drop by his office sometimes, too, especially if Barranco was lurking around. Joshua's father never harassed her when Gaede — more than twice Barranco's size — was nearby. If her ex-boyfriend assumed she and Gaede were dating, that was just fine with Fruge.

That Valentine's Day, Gaede surprised Fruge by sending her a dozen roses and an adorable stuffed animal for Joshua. Still, when Gaede actually asked her out, Fruge hedged. Joshua was with his dad that weekend, but Fruge told Gaede she couldn't leave the teen-age Raychel home alone. Gaede suggested Raychel come along, and the three had a great time at Red Lobster.

Raychel had taken her parents' divorce badly. Barranco, too, had inflicted emotional damage upon her. Since her parents split up, Raychel had become a far sadder girl than she once was, and she shared her mother's teen-age weight problem. Gaede drew Raychel out of her depression almost immediately. She became attached to him quickly. Fruge could see her daughter's self-esteem skyrocket within a short time after Gaede entered their lives. "He's great," Raychel told her mother early on. "He's the first one of your boyfriends I've ever liked."

Joshua also liked "Daddy Dennis." The boy would howl with glee when Gaede wrapped him in a bear hug, complete with growling animal sound effects. Gaede did his best to talk and sing in Spanish, which Joshua used at Barranco's house. Gaede's Spanish wasn't good, and he laughed at himself when the 3-year-old corrected him.

Within two months, Gaede told Fruge: "I'm going to marry you."

"What makes you think that?" she asked.

"Because I want to," he replied.

"Do you always get what you want?" she asked.

"Usually," he said.

Gaede promised Fruge that after they married, she could quit working and stay home with the kids. He took her, Raychel and Joshua on a weekend trip to Fargo, describing it as a nice place to raise kids because of the low crime rate. The allure of no longer being a single parent, along with Gaede's charm, made up for his failings in the looks department. True to his prediction, the two were married May 1, 2001. The civil ceremony took place at the Milwaukee County Courthouse, and Gaede filled the room with roses.

After a family dinner at the Chancery, a neighborhood restaurant and bar, the newlyweds set off on their honeymoon.

Because money was tight and Fruge didn't want to spend too much time away from her kids, Gaede suggested they drive northwest to Tomah, where he had once lived. Gaede wore a pricey platinum wedding band and a $1,200 Esquire watch, but the couple spent their first night as husband and wife at the EconoLodge.

When they woke up the next morning, their car was gone. Gaede seemed paranoid about calling the police due to some of his past history in the town, but Fruge insisted. The good news was that the police had found their car. The bad news was that the vehicle was in an impound lot, and the officers were unwilling to take them to it. Gaede and Fruge had to rent a car to get there, an expense not in their budget.

Back at the hotel, Fruge was cutting up some food when her hand slipped and she sliced her finger open. The blood wouldn't stop, so they were off to the hospital so she could get stitches. At the time, Fruge chalked it up to bad luck. In hindsight, she realized she should have taken it as an omen.

CHAPTER NINE

A month after Fruge and Gaede married, he was arrested for non-payment of child support. By then, he owed his ex-wife, Lorelie, some $40,000. Gaede was picked up by the police after he didn't show up for a court date in the case. He claimed the process server gave the summons to his mother, Hazel, in Milwaukee, and she'd never told him about it.

The judge set bond at $10,000 and then reduced it to $5,000 when Gaede couldn't pay. Unfortunately, he and Fruge didn't even have that amount, so he sat in jail for about a month. When the new court date finally arrived, the judge let Gaede out on bond after he paid $500 and promised to send Lorelie support checks regularly.

As a precaution, the county's child support enforcement division planned to withhold money from his paychecks. Gaede listed Lodis Financial Group as his employer and Diana Fruge as his boss. Authorities didn't know Lodis was his own business, nor did they know Fruge was his wife. Needless to say, child support money wasn't taken out of his checks.

Shortly after Gaede got out of jail on the child support charges, he told his bride he'd been charged with two felonies back in 1995 in Monroe County, the same area where they had gone on their honeymoon. He had fled, but thanks to the child support mess, the cops had figured out where he was. He swore he was not guilty, and Fruge believed he'd be acquitted. She drove with him to the courthouse in Sparta for the trial in late July 2001, but she had to wait in the hall because the bailiff wouldn't let Joshua into the courtroom. The trial took less than a day. Gaede was convicted of being a party to the crimes of aiding a felon and escape.

Despite the fact that Gaede had jumped bail once before — shortly after the charges had been issued six years earlier — the judge allowed him to be freed on $10,000 bail pending sentencing. To be released, he only had to put up 10 percent of that. It stretched the new family's resources to their limits, but Gaede told his new wife there was no way he was going back to the Monroe County Jail. Everyone was out to get him in that part of the state, he said. Prosecutors, bikers and cops held grudges, and they wanted him dead. That's why he'd fled before, and that's why he had to run again. This time, he would take his family with him.

He knew exactly where he wanted to go: North Dakota. Gaede's desire to relocate to Fargo because of the low crime rate was ironic, considering that he had personally helped raise the crime rate practically everywhere he lived.

He had also worked on the other side of the law as an undercover officer. According to Gaede, it all started in 1987, when a detective told him: "Here's your opportunity to turn this felony into a simple mistake, and everybody goes home happy."

Gaede was living in his native Milwaukee, married to his high school sweetheart, Lorelie Rodefer. They had started dating when they were 16 and married three years later, shortly after high school graduation. By 1987, their two young children were thriving, he said. Gaede operated his own garage, where he worked on cars and operated a tow truck. He tooled around on a Harley Davidson motorcycle, sometimes with his 4-year-old daughter on the back. He hung out at a popular biker bar. Some weekends, the family went to their farm in Monroe County's Tomah, about a 170-mile drive from Milwaukee.

The threatened felony charge resulted from a bad investment in some used tow truck parts, Gaede said. As it turned out, the parts were stolen. He jumped at the chance to make the felony go away. The police wanted information on some of the patrons at the biker bar, and Gaede was more than happy to provide it. The bikers never caught on, as far as he could tell.

Gaede said he wanted to stay on the good side of the law, so he signed up for police science classes at Waukesha County Technical College, just west of Milwaukee. He continued to work as a paid informant for the West Allis Police Department. Everyone there knew he wanted to be a cop. His information was always reliable, and he even typed up all his own reports.

In time, Gaede became an undercover operative for the West Central Metropolitan Enforcement Group, a regional vice task force. Although he wasn't a sworn officer, Gaede operated like one, infiltrating drug gangs and motorcycle clubs that were fronts for narcotics and violence. Gaede's weekend work often led him 200 miles northwest of Milwaukee to Black River Falls. With a tattoo of a skull and a musical note on his left bicep, he was always an imposing figure, whether or not he wore his leather motorcycle jacket.

One night in December 1990, Gaede said, he made his biggest bust of all, and records detail his version of events. He had no way of knowing that a night out with Lorelie and an attempt to get rid of someone he considered a shady cop would lead to nothing but trouble.

Gaede and his wife were hanging out at Pete's Keg and Kettle with some friends, Jerry Stolfi and Rick Dorn. On the other side of the bar, off-duty Jackson County Sheriff's Deputy James Haldeman was having a drink with his brother-in-law. Haldeman approached Gaede's group politely at first, shaking hands and introducing himself. Haldeman had been with the sheriff's department since 1972, and he'd received numerous commendations for his work.

During Haldeman's first dozen years on the job, his record was spotless. His first departmental discipline came in 1984, after he fired a department shotgun at a grouse, missing the bird and damaging a barn in the process. He'd been suspended for a single day.

Later in the '80s, Haldeman got into more trouble. In 1985, he reportedly conducted an illegal search for drugs

71

without a warrant and then filed a false report about the incident. In 1987, there was another illegal search, this time for a missing tool and die set. Haldeman found the missing items, but because he hadn't followed the letter of the law, he told the victim of the theft not to tell anyone. That same year, he continued interrogating a suspect after the man had invoked his right to remain silent. Those offenses combined yielded Haldeman a 45-day suspension without pay. By 1990, Haldeman's formerly stellar career was on a downslide.

On the night at Pete's Keg and Kettle, it didn't take the off-duty detective in the red windbreaker long to approach Gaede's group. "Do you own a Harley?" he asked Gaede, who was wearing the motorcycle jacket.

Gaede told Haldeman he did. The more they talked, the closer Haldeman got to Lorelie. He put his arm around her and when she ignored him, he lowered his hand to her backside.

Lorelie elbowed him away.

"I better move before I get slapped," Haldeman said.

"I hit harder than she does," Gaede replied.

Haldeman pointed to the motorcycle club emblem on Gaede's jacket. "This scares me," he said. Then he formally introduced himself as a law enforcement officer.

"Do you know Rick Pomeroy and Mike Homegreen?" Gaede asked, throwing out the names of some of the contacts in his own operation.

"They're dickheads, and you're dirty," Haldeman replied.

Gaede figured it was safe to tell Haldeman, another cop, that he worked for the drug unit.

"You mean I could have just sold you some pot, and I would have been arrested by my own people?" Haldeman asked incredulously. He warned Gaede not to reveal his undercover status so easily, then abruptly made his way back to his brother-in-law.

Gaede could see Haldeman pointing at him, effectively blowing his cover. In Gaede's opinion, Haldeman was drunk, disorderly and a dirty cop. The next day, Gaede filed a complaint against Haldeman, which resulted in a five-day suspension. Haldeman, in turn, filed a grievance protesting the suspension.

Gaede didn't expect retribution. A suspension alone probably wouldn't have been enough to warrant Haldeman's lifelong rancor. But for the 18-year veteran detective, Gaede's complaint was the beginning of the end of his police career, arbitration records show.

About a year before the incident at Pete's, Haldeman was assigned to investigate the murder, rape and torture of a 9-year-old girl named Jennifer Wesho, who lived on a Jackson County Indian reservation. Haldeman was accused of mishandling the investigation, and the results were disastrous.

A reserve officer who had been assisting in the case got a confession from a young girl, who admitted she and several others had killed Wesho. Instead of placing the report in the department file, Haldeman kept it in his own private files. Then Haldeman personally interviewed the girl. Again, he never put his notes in the department file. Haldeman then interviewed a boy allegedly involved in the crime. A third person was implicated during the interview and ultimately charged.

Haldeman never had the tape of the boy's interview transcribed. He put the tape into his personal files and didn't make it part of the department's main investigative record on the Wesho case.

No one found out about the improprieties until late April 1991, when a defense attorney presented evidence of them in court. The district attorney was forced to drop the murder charges. Haldeman was fired for botching the investigation. Haldeman's union lawyer claimed the detective had never attempted to hide information in the Wesho case.

Haldeman, the lawyer argued, "became the scapegoat for a bungled job out of the District Attorney's office."

At the time he was fired, Haldeman's grievance for the suspension due to his actions at Pete's Keg and Kettle was still pending. Both the suspension and the firing were considered during the same arbitration hearing in the summer of 1991. The arbitrator, attorney Amedo Greco, upheld the suspension and the firing. He also had some harsh words regarding Haldeman's treatment of Lorelie. "Haldeman's pawing of her, which she deeply resented by elbowing him away, was unprofessional and totally uncalled for," Greco wrote. "The same was true of his overbearing and hostile questioning (of Gaede), which was reinforced by his disclosing that he was a law enforcement officer. Haldeman had no business whatsoever in engaging in such questioning, and he ... was primarily responsible for the unpleasantness which followed."

In finding the firing appropriate, Greco noted that Haldeman's negligence in the Wesho case "was part of an ongoing pattern of misconduct which showed no sign of otherwise letting up."

Might Haldeman have been fired for his handling of the Wesho case even if he had never met Dennis Gaede? Maybe. Nonetheless, Gaede feared that he had just made a formidable enemy. Gaede decided it would be wise to stay out of Jackson County, knowing that fallen officers can have powerful friends.

Although Gaede never finished the course work for a police science degree, he figured his undercover experience could help him get a law enforcement job without one. He was right. In 1991, the police department in Marshfield (about a 220-mile drive from Milwaukee) hired him to work undercover drug cases. His job there ended badly, with Gaede pleading no contest to two misdemeanors: cocaine possession and obstructing an officer. He served 90 days in jail.

"I remember him promising a lot of things, but within a short period of time, we came to realize he was a blowhard and was not able to deliver on the promises he made," said Marshfield Police Chief Joseph Stoik. "The only conviction he got us was himself."

After he got out of jail, Gaede said, he lived in the woods and worked at a car dealership. His probation was revoked for buying a Porsche without his probation officer's permission, he said. So it was back to jail for another four or five months.

According to Gaede, the defense attorney who represented him on the revocation warned him yet again: "You've got to get out of here. These people are going to kill you."

Gaede's personal life was falling apart, too. In 1995, after 13 years of marriage, Lorelie filed for divorce, claiming her husband had been emotionally abusive to her. Gaede claimed the divorce occurred because she had cheated on him while he was in jail.

"Then she went to court and said I was giving (the kids) drugs and alcohol," he said. Gaede hired a lawyer and tried to fight for custody of Lindsey, who was 11 by then and loved riding on the back of his Harley; and Devin, two years younger. But Gaede couldn't pay the lawyer's fees, and the judge allowed the attorney to withdraw from the case.

The couple went to mediation. As a result, joint legal custody was granted. Gaede agreed to let the children live most of the time with their mother. They would spend time with him on school breaks and weekends, and they would always stay with him over Labor Day and Memorial Day.

Their father was not allowed to take the children out of the state, and they were prohibited from spending the night with Gaede's mother, Hazel. Gaede also was ordered to pay child support of $125 a week or 25 percent of his income, whichever was more.

As the divorce proceeded, Gaede moved again. This time, he settled in Sparta, about 80 miles north of Marshfield. He figured it was far enough away to stay out of trouble with his former employers, but close enough to visit his kids. For a time, he again worked selling cars. Then, with financial help from his mother, Gaede opened Big Dee's Restaurant, housed in the American Legion Hall.

Big Dee's Restaurant was a family place with a bar and an extensive menu, despite its small kitchen. Gaede said he did a lot of the cooking himself. He started spending more and more time with a waitress named Robin. She was younger than his ex-wife, more stylish, more hip. They started seeing each other. At the same time, Gaede went back to collecting information about bad bikers, this time for the Monroe County Sheriff's Department.

"Because of the people that I knew, I was swept right into this and I didn't look back," Gaede said. It was the beginning of the case that would finally go to trial some six years later, after Gaede had married Fruge.

When Gaede's contacts in the department asked him to hire a jail inmate on work release, he agreed, Gaede said. Looking back, he said he's convinced it was a setup. The police were trying to bring him down, he said, because he had gone back to investigating dirty cops and because he'd found evidence that a cop and a prosecutor were involved with drugs, and maybe with a murder.

Monroe County District Attorney Dan Cary said Gaede was the one who volunteered to give the inmate a job. The rest of Gaede's allegations were "ludicrous," Cary said. "I certainly don't believe there was any kind of a setup. I find that kind of ridiculous," he said.

In any event, the inmate fled during his first day on the job, and Gaede found himself charged with being party to the crimes of aiding a felon and escape. The officials he accused of wrongdoing, whom he said he's still afraid of naming publicly, were never charged.

Gaede said he had been planning a Mexican night at the restaurant with tamales, margaritas and other south-of-the-border delicacies. He drove to the nearby town of La-Crosse to buy some fresh corn husks. By the time he got back, the work release inmate was gone. Gaede laughed when he was hauled in to court for aiding an escape. "You've got to be kidding," he told the authorities. They were dead serious. The criminal complaint in the case said Gaede drove the inmate to a casino on an Indian reservation as part of a plan to help him escape. On reservations, state and county authorities have no jurisdiction, and it's unlikely that the FBI would come after a small-time criminal who was hiding out there.

Gaede was released on his own recognizance while the case was pending but ordered to report to the jail every morning. He did so dutifully, Gaede said, until the bikers he'd ratted on somehow found out what he'd done and came after him. It all started with a visit from one of the guys he had busted. The man showed up outside the restaurant with a disposable camera and a canister of pepper spray. He snapped Gaede's picture and promised to send it to every member of the wronged motorcycle club he could find.

Gaede tried to explain. "I never tried to bust you," he said. "I'm not working with law enforcement anymore." By the end of the conversation, Gaede felt he had convinced the guy he was telling the truth. The two shook hands, and the guy drove away.

Later that night, though, Gaede's telephone rang. "Hey motherfucker, how you doing?" the caller asked. "How long of a tail do rats have?" The caller's diatribe ended with a threat: "We're going to burn that house down with you in it."

Gaede was up all night. When he went to the police the next morning, they were unwilling to help, he said.

That's when he thought of Canada. The Monroe County authorities had no jurisdiction there, and Gaede had at least one friend in Winnipeg he could turn to. Several years before, during a motorcycle fund-raiser for Easter Seals in Milwaukee, Gaede had met a group of Canadian bikers. They had planned to stay in town after the big ride, camping and taking part in the festivities. They had their camping gear but hadn't reserved a camp site. They told Gaede about their plight, and he let them camp in his backyard. If Gaede ever came to Canada, they told him on their way out of town, he should look them up.

As an added bonus, the Canadian bikers were longtime rivals of the ones who were chasing him. Gaede thought it unlikely that his pursuers would look for him in enemy territory.

When Gaede told Robin he had to leave, she seemed to understand. Her brother was involved with a gang, he said, so she knew all about self-preservation. Gaede packed his stuff and headed north on Thanksgiving day, 1995.

Gaede didn't find out until 2000 that Robin had been pregnant with his daughter when he left. A courtroom deputy at the escape trial informed Gaede that Robin had shown up, pursuing a paternity case. Gaede didn't believe it and planned to fight it all the way — until he saw Alyssa. "She looked like one of our family," he said.

CHAPTER TEN

Gaede always had an affinity for Laurie Bembenek, the beautiful Milwaukee cop turned convicted murderer. Despite his training in law enforcement, Gaede couldn't help rooting for Bembenek in 1990 when she escaped from a Wisconsin prison and went on the lam in Canada. He'd even plastered a "Run, Bambi, Run" bumper sticker on his car. But he wouldn't make the mistake of heading for Thunder Bay the way Bambi had. Gaede was going to Winnipeg.

For two years, Gaede said, he lived quietly under his own name. He was happy to be away from vengeful bikers and dirty cops. Then in 1995, he said, his sister Sue called to warn him that another sister, Kathy, had figured out where he was hiding. Kathy had found one of the many Western Union receipts that had piled up in Hazel's car when she sent her son money. Kathy's husband was tight with one of the biker gangs who was after Gaede, he said. She felt more loyalty to her husband than her brother and planned to rat him out. Gaede had to disappear again.

Gaede was a marked man, so he had to become someone else, he said. One of his friends introduced him to a retired motorcycle clubber who knew all about living in disguise, he said. The identity the man gave Gaede belonged to Grant Devon Lindblom, a child who had died in 1963 at the age of 5. Gaede managed to get a birth certificate in Lindblom's name. Once he had done that, it was easy to get a Canadian passport, a Manitoba driver's license and a social insurance number, which gave him access to Canada's nationalized health care system. He also got a couple of credit cards.

Living as Grant Devon Lindblom, Gaede blended seamlessly into the Winnipeg community. He befriended a guitarist, and the two of them recruited three other guys to start a rock and heavy metal band called Widow. They even cut a CD.

Gaede went back to school, attending an 18-month program in business administration at Herzing College. When he began to suspect the school wasn't paying the proper licensing fees for some software programs, he reported it to Microsoft — with no regard for the possibility that he might draw attention to himself. His concerns about the licensing turned out to be unfounded, but the school administration's negative reaction to his complaints was merely a small blemish on his new life.

Gaede asked his new friends to call him Devon. Although it was spelled differently, Gaede was happy that his assumed name could be pronounced the same as the one he'd given his son back in Wisconsin a lifetime ago.

Devon and his band's guitarist, Chris Davis, were out at a popular '70s club called the Boogie Nights Cabaret the night he met 21-year-old Tannis Fleming. The house band wore bell bottoms and sported colored afros, and disco was king.

Tannis and a friend of hers were at the club and knew Davis. They came over to say hello, Gaede said. He said he wasn't looking for a girlfriend, but Tannis was sweet and persistent.

Rail-thin with long, straight dark hair she often wore in a bun, Tannis was never popular in school. The other kids teased her a lot because she was so skinny, which gave Tannis "a lot of complexes," her mother said. The girl also lacked self-confidence. Three years after graduating from high school, Tannis lived with her parents. Her social circle consisted of one friend and a look-alike cousin. Her love life was practically non-existent.

On the night she met Gaede in 1997, Tannis didn't have a job. As she had throughout her youth, she spent much of her time taking care of her younger brother, who had Down Syndrome. Her goal in life was to marry a good man who would take care of her. Once she found her prince, she hoped they would have lots of children.

It wasn't difficult for Widow's drummer to sweep the shy, gullible Tannis off her feet. After just three or four dates, she brought him home to meet her family. Her mother, Joanne, was already in bed by the time they arrived. "You've got company," Joanne's husband, Rick, said, shaking her. "I think you want to get up."

Joanne pulled herself together and went to meet her daughter's beau, who introduced himself as Devon. His huge girth was a sharp contrast to Tannis' slim figure. Personality-wise, too, they were polar opposites. Devon was loud and gregarious. He talked big, telling Joanne he had once played the drums on a cruise ship with '80s rock legend Joan Jett, although he didn't have any pictures or recordings to back up the story. His agent, he said, had recommended he come to Canada and start a band.

Within three months, Devon and Tannis had moved into a basement apartment together. Three months after that, she was pregnant. Their son, Dylan, was born in August 1999. By that time, the two were engaged, ring and all. Devon told his future in-laws it would be his second marriage.

"I thought, 'Well, it's a bit quick, but whatever,'" Joanne recalled.

At that time, Joanne's only concern about her future son-in-law was where he got his money. Devon was a big spender, always wining and dining Tannis and giving her gifts. Devon claimed to have the best of everything back in the States: a camper, a cabin, investments. Yet in Winnipeg, he never seemed able to hold a job longer than a few months. He worked as an accountant and a car salesman. He had even started his own company, called North Star Distributors. The company consisted of a small refrigerated truck from which he sold exotic meats. His favorites were jerky sticks made from alligator and kangaroo.

"I'm an entrepreneur," he explained. "And I find people to work with me."

Joanne finally found out her daughter's betrothed was getting a lot of money from his mother. She found that slightly unusual, considering that he was 34 at the time. When Joanne asked Devon about it, he told her he owned two businesses back in Wisconsin, a towing company and a restaurant. The money his mother sent, he said, was merely his portion of the proceeds.

But the more Joanne got to know Devon, the less she trusted him. Whenever the family got together for a holiday or birthday celebration, Devon, sick or exhausted, holed up in a bedroom. One time, when Devon and Tannis had planned to go camping with her parents, Joanne took down the license number of Devon's van.

"He saw me and he freaked right out," Joanne recalled.

She explained to Devon that she needed the number for security in case they became separated. The explanation seemed to pacify him.

"Something's not right about him," Joanne told her husband later.

"I think you just worry too much," he replied.

Many times, Joanne became skeptical of Devon's claims. But every time she questioned him, he had an explanation and solid proof. One day, Joanne and Tannis were playing cards, talking about a friend who was in training to join the Royal Canadian Mounted Police.

"You know, I used to be an undercover narcotics officer," Devon told his future mother-in-law.

"Yeah, right," she replied. "You're full of shit."

He pulled out a pen with the name of a police department on it, and then flipped over the lapel of his jacket to reveal an embroidered police department patch.

Devon also claimed he had worked as a paramedic. Yet two months after their son was born, Tannis went into diabetic shock. Devon called an ambulance, but didn't do any emergency first aid in the meantime.

"Why didn't you give her first aid?" Joanne asked Devon later.

"I panicked," he replied.

"I don't think you were a paramedic," she challenged him.

Devon pulled out another identification card. He flashed it quickly, but she could see that it read, "Curtis Ambulance Service." It had his picture on it.

Another time, when Joanne was baby-sitting her grandson, she came across a letter addressed to Devon Gareau.

"Who's this?" she asked him.

"That's my stage name," he explained. "You know, the one I use with the band."

Despite Joanne's misgivings, the wedding was set for June 16, 2000.

Although Dylan would be nearly 2 by the time the big day arrived, his father's family in the States had never met him. As the wedding approached, Joanne decided she wanted Devon's family to meet the boy ahead of time. Although Dylan hadn't yet been diagnosed as autistic, his parents, as well as Rick and Joanne, had started to suspect something was wrong. They didn't want any of Devon's relatives to be surprised.

"My mom doesn't have a lot of money," Devon said when Joanne broached the idea.

"Well, why don't we plan a trip to Milwaukee, then," she suggested. "Because I really want to meet her."

Despite Devon's warnings that Milwaukee was too dangerous, Tannis' parents and her two brothers made the trip in their camper. Devon had just started a new job and said he couldn't get the time off work to join them. Tannis stayed behind as well.

Joanne says she wasn't impressed with Devon's mother, Hazel, who seemed cold and uninterested in her

83

grandson. On the other hand, Devon's sister, Sue, was warm and sweet, and took to her nephew immediately. Joanne was glad she had made the trip.

When the Flemings returned to Winnipeg, plans for the wedding celebration were in full swing. The civil ceremony would be officiated by a friend of the family, a woman who worked for the government and had the same authority to perform a wedding as an American justice of the peace.

"The first thing she asked me was had he been married before," Joanne recalled. "I said yes, and she said, 'I need a copy of his divorce papers.'"

Devon ranted and raved, Joanne said. He seemed unwilling to go back to the States and dig through his files for the documents.

"I'm giving you until the end of February," Joanne told him. "If I don't have them by then, I'm canceling everything."

So Devon went to Wisconsin and returned with papers confirming the dissolution of the marriage of Grant Devon Lindblom and Lorelie Rodefer. At the time, neither Joanne nor the woman who was to perform the ceremony had any idea the documents were forged.

By February, the Flemings had invested about $2,500 in Tannis' dream wedding. It would be an outdoor ceremony at Joanne's brother's place, five acres along the river. Guests would be invited to bring their campers and stay the weekend, and many had already told Joanne they planned to do so. Joanne had rented tents for the dinner and dancing. Tannis would have two bridesmaids, her best friend and her cousin. Devon's best man was coming up from Milwaukee.

But the wedding never happened.

Gaede said his new life began to unravel the day he applied for a student loan to help pay his business school tuition. The man in the student loan office typed his assumed name and identification number into a computer. "You're dead," he told Gaede.

"Huh?" Gaede asked. Gaede said something about how he couldn't be dead, he was standing right there.

The man in front of the computer didn't seem concerned and blamed a software glitch. Gaede, though, got nervous. Thinking back, Gaede figured the loan officer must have been the one who called in an anonymous tip about his whereabouts a few days later. He was wrong.

Gaede's would-be mother-in-law was the one who gave his secrets away. Joanne recalls the day vividly. She and Tannis had just paid off the wedding gown. Tannis looked radiant in the simple but elegant gown, white satin on top and lace on the bottom. The matching veil had been her mother's. They had the netting shortened and fastened to a new, more modern headpiece.

Joanne had begun to put her misgivings aside and hope her daughter really would live happily ever after. She could imagine her daughter and the bridesmaids walking down the aisle with the silk flower bouquets Joanne had made: yellow roses for Tannis, pink roses for the bridesmaids.

The night after they paid off the dress, Joanne was assembling matching boutonnieres. In the midst of her work, the phone rang. It was one of the guests from Devon's side of the family. She said she couldn't make the wedding. She gave the excuse that her manager at work wouldn't give her the time off. Joanne pressed her.

Finally, the woman broke down. "I can't live with this anymore," Joanne recalls her saying. "You're good people, and I don't want to see you get hurt." She told Joanne that Devon wasn't who he seemed. His real name, the woman said, was Dennis Gaede, and he was a wanted criminal in the United States.

Joanne, acting as an anonymous tipster, called the police. She couldn't bring herself to tell Tannis the truth until six months later.

A few days after Joanne phoned in the tip, in early March 2000, at around 7 a.m., the police came to the door of the apartment Tannis and the man she knew as Grant Devon Lindblom shared. They told Tannis they needed to speak to Grant Lindblom about a car insurance claim.

"He's sleeping," she told them.

"Wake him up," they instructed.

The police told him they knew he was Dennis Gaede. He was in trouble, they said, and not only for stealing a dead boy's identity in Canada. The Monroe County, Wisconsin, authorities had a warrant out for his arrest for helping someone escape. He would be deported, and American officials planned to take him into custody as soon as he crossed into the United States.

According to the warrant, Gaede had called the jail and volunteered to give the inmate a job as part of a sophisticated escape plan. The warrant also said he should be considered "armed and dangerous."

As Gaede was led away, Tannis panicked. "He's not Dennis, he's Devon," she insisted over and over. She never saw him again.

According to Gaede, he was charged with passport forgery and obtaining credit cards under false pretenses, but the Canadian authorities didn't bother prosecuting him. Instead, Gaede said, he was quickly deported.

As soon as his legal problems in the United States were resolved, Gaede planned to call a lawyer right away, to see if there was a there was a way he could get back to Canada, back to his fiancée and his son. Tannis couldn't move south, he said, because she had a lot of health problems and there was no way she could afford the medical treatments for them if she left Canada's nationalized health care system.

Gaede said he crossed the border out of Canada alone and entered the United States in the tiny town of Pembina, North Dakota. To his surprise, there were no cops waiting to arrest him on the other side. There was no one.

He walked along the road until he came to a church. Gaede said the minister, whose name he can't recall, fed him and let him stay the night. The next morning, the minister gave him a bus ticket to Milwaukee and a duffle bag. When Gaede looked inside, he found a six-pack of Budweiser and half a bottle of Jack Daniels. It was March 2000. That's when Gaede decided he really liked North Dakota.

CHAPTER ELEVEN

When Fargo Investigator Tammy Lynk looked into Gaede's past, she hit pay dirt almost immediately. She found records of his November 1999 arrest in Canada on charges of "passport forgery" and "false pretense — obtain credit cards." The Canadian police report said Gaede obtained the birth certificate of a dead child in May 1997, and then applied for a social insurance number and passport in the child's name. Canadian authorities had seized a driver's license, a social insurance card, a passport and two credit cards: a Bank of Montreal Master Card and a Peoples/Mappins credit card.

Gaede had used at least three aliases in Canada: Grant Lindblum, Grant Gareau and Grant Devon Lindblom. Canadian authorities had established his true identity through fingerprints.

The Canadian report seemed to fit with the suspicions Lynk now had about Gaede stealing Wicks' identity. There was just one major difference: In Canada, Gaede had used the identities of people who were already dead. In Fargo, the man whose identity he'd used had turned up dead afterwards.

As soon as Lynk scrutinized the résumé "Wicks" had used to get hired at Compressed Air, it became clear that no one had done a thorough background check. His references were suspect. The phone for Lodis Financial Group had been disconnected. The number for Incotax, Inc. rang and rang, but no one answered. North Star Distributors and Al's Tax Service came up empty. At the Zoological society of Manitoba, the man Wicks had listed as his supervisor had since died. The Spherion interviewer's notes on Wicks' application noted that the Zoological Society "can't assist much — too long ago."

By mid-January 2002, Maxwell and Paridon of Compressed Air Technologies had figured out that their former bookkeeper had embezzled some $20,000 from their company. The knowledge hit Maxwell like he'd fallen backwards off a ladder. He didn't realize he'd dodged an even more lethal bullet.

Shortly after noon on January 24, the man Maxwell and Paridon knew as Wicks called to see if his ex-bosses would be willing to accept items from his Gardner home as restitution for the embezzled money. The answer: Maybe. Maxwell and Paridon asked the man if he would meet them at the house to work things out. "I can't," he said, and hung up.

As Maxwell and Paridon delved more deeply into the last days of their bookkeeper's employment, they found more and more problems. Wicks, who they now knew was Gaede, had signed up his family for the company's health insurance before his eligibility date and deducted the entire cost from the company account. He hadn't paid a single employee contribution. He'd purchased two cell phones and paid the bills through the company. When doing the payroll, he'd regularly added $50 per week to his check. He'd even given himself a $100 Christmas bonus.

Paridon recalled asking his bookkeeper about a check for $50 made payable to Dawson Insurance. Gaede seemed apologetic. "It was for my homeowners' insurance," he said. "I was going to pay it back." Gaede told his boss that the insurance company would only accept a check from a business, not a personal check.

The story was fishy, but Paridon couldn't prove it was false. Lynk could. Jan Johnson of Dawson Insurance told Lynk the $50 payment was for a $7,500 bond. Gaede said he needed the bond in order to become a notary public. Johnson faxed Lynk a copy of the bond application and told the investigator neither Wicks nor Gaede bought homeowners' insurance from her company. Paridon said there was no reason Gaede would need notary public status to perform his job at Compressed Air.

90

Another Compressed Air employee told the Fargo police that even though Paridon had denied Gaede permission on that cold winter day, he had used one of Compressed Air's trucks anyway. When Paridon and Maxwell searched the truck, a Sawzall turned up missing.

A Sawzall is a high-powered, battery operated reciprocating saw. Marketing materials refer to the tool as "a hatchet kit" that can be used for "aggressive wood cutting." It is effective, another sales pitch says, when other tools are useless.

*   *   *

Gaede and Fruge's rental application for the duplex where they'd first lived after moving to Fargo provided Lynk with more useful information. Their previous address was an apartment in West Allis, Wisconsin. Fruge had listed a previous employer as Bieck Management. Fruge had served as a resident manager at one of their apartment buildings. However, Fruge had left the apartment and the job without notifying her bosses. Lynk would not learn the rest of the story until years later.

Although the abrupt departure from West Allis had not been Fruge's idea, she had not argued with her new husband about it. Gaede told her that if he stuck around for sentencing on the old escape case and ended up in a Wisconsin prison, Haldeman's buddies would kill him. North Dakota was a small state, with a population of only about 600,000. With its low crime rate, Gaede said, they would be safe there.

Getting out of Milwaukee was also appealing to Fruge because it would get her away from Barranco once and for all. Joshua's father was giving her nothing but grief, and she was tired of dealing with it. She knew it would be illegal to violate their custody agreement and take Joshua away, but she told herself the boy would be better off in the long run.

The only alternative was to go back to the life of a single parent, and Fruge didn't want that. She couldn't bear the thought of living without her husband, and she was terrified at the possibility of seeing him thrown in prison or worse. Fruge's teenage daughter, Raychel, would move in with her dad. The rest of the family would get out of town.

At first, life in North Dakota was idyllic. Gaede began using Wicks' name, assuring his wife the naïve drummer from Hales Corners would never find out. Fruge refused to call herself Mrs. Wicks. Instead, she gave up Gaede's last name and went back to her first husband's name, Fruge, which she had used for most of her adult life. If people in Fargo thought she and Gaede/Wicks were shacking up, she didn't care. Gaede agreed to the arrangement.

Living in Fargo as Wicks, Gaede felt safe and certain that his family would stay hidden. The bookkeeping job at Compressed Air seemed a perfect fit. Fruge fell in love with their aging blue farmhouse. It seemed like the beginning of the white picket fence life that Gaede had promised her when they married.

For a time, Fruge worked at Camelot Cleaners, but she burned her arm on a piece of equipment and quit. She put in a few hours at Compressed Air after Paridon and Maxwell gave her some money to pay her attorney, but soon found she was in over her head with their computer system.

As time went by, Fruge decided Gardner was just too small and remote. No one would deliver a pizza to their farmhouse, and the bartender at the Happy Hour Tap down the street didn't know how to make a martini.

Fruge missed her daughter. She missed her mother, her sisters and her friends in Milwaukee. She puttered around the farmhouse in the town she'd taken to calling Petticoat Junction, cleaning, unpacking and re-arranging. During the day, with only Joshua for company, Fruge felt isolated and alone. Gaede had warned her not to get too friendly with the neighbors, who could blow the whole plan if they got nosy.

Fruge fell back on her favorite hobby: drinking. It was beer at first, then Mike's Hard Lemonade, then all the hard liquor she could get her hands on. Gaede was her soul mate, her partner, the love of her life, but even that wasn't enough. Fruge needed friends. She needed adventure. She just plain needed something to do.

One day Gaede stopped at the mall and bought his wife a diamond ring and a necklace with a heart-shaped pendant and tanzanite stone from the Zales jewelry store. At first, she was thrilled. Then, she became disturbed by how much he talked about the jewelry store manager, a blond woman who was also married. Gaede would come home late from work, and his wife would discover he had been having drinks with the woman at the mall. Gaede eventually told Fruge the woman had propositioned him, but he had turned her down.

Fruge flew into a drunken rage, convinced that her husband, the only person in the entire state of North Dakota whom she could count on, was cheating on her. Gaede had his wife committed to an in-patient alcohol treatment program. The majority of the cost for the week in rehab at Prairie St. John's, a psychiatric hospital, was paid for through his health insurance at Compressed Air.

Back at home, Fruge's outlook improved slightly. She bought non-alcoholic beer to satisfy her cravings, staying away from the real thing. But then Gaede's bosses at Compressed Air started asking questions about their accounts and Paridon snapped Gaede's picture. Gaede knew it was only a matter of time before the police would come calling. He couldn't hide his trepidation from his wife.

When he received the call from Lynk asking about the books at Compressed Air, Gaede wasn't surprised, and he kept his cool. He promised to come to the station with evidence that Compressed Air's founders were cheating on their taxes. Fruge says Gaede knew he couldn't really do that. If the police investigator didn't believe his tale, he'd be charged with stealing. Worse, it was only a matter of time before someone who knew him saw that photo and realized he wasn't Tim Wicks.

"I might have to kill him," Fruge recalled Gaede saying.

She thought it was pure hyperbole. Gaede went on, talking about a plan to get Wicks relocated to Canada. That way, there would be less chance of anyone finding out Gaede was the one who had stolen Wicks' identity. In the weeks that followed, Gaede called the real Wicks and suggested they get together to play a gig in Winnipeg, Fruge said. When Wicks disappeared and more police started asking questions, Gaede got nervous.

Fruge recalled those days in late 2001 and early 2002 as a crazy time. At one point, when Gaede left her alone with Joshua for two or three days, Fruge called Barranco in desperation. "You've got to wire me some money," she begged. "Dennis has gone crazy." Fruge told her son's father that Gaede was abusing her and she feared for Joshua's safety. She would bring the boy back to Wisconsin, Fruge promised, if Barranco would wire $500 to her.

Barranco promised to scrape together as much cash as he could. Fruge put Joshua into the aging blue Buick Hazel had given them and drove the 20 miles to Fargo. When the wire transfer arrived at the Sun Mart grocery store, Fruge felt momentary relief, and then renewed frustration. Barranco had sent just $50. That was nowhere near enough for a woman and a toddler alone on a 600-mile road trip.

Defeated, she drove back to Gardner, opened a beer and waited for her husband to return.

When Gaede got back about two days later, he had a plan. They would head for Canada. Gaede had been happy there once before, and he thought they could start over there.

First, though, they had some business to attend to in Milwaukee. Gaede wanted to stop by his mother's Laundromat to say goodbye. He also had a few items he needed to leave with her.

Joshua had a court-ordered visit scheduled with his father, so Fruge took him to Barranco's place for that. Childless for a couple of days, Gaede and Fruge checked into the Park Motel on 27th Street. From there, they drove to the Hoan Bridge.

A sewage plant lies on the south end of the Hoan Bridge. On the north, there is a summer festival grounds. To the local population, the Hoan is known as "the bridge to nowhere." It's also known as a good place to lose things. It wasn't uncommon for cops who couldn't find a murder weapon to shrug and say, "He probably threw it off the Hoan Bridge." Items thrown from the bridge are seldom found. In heavy rains, sewage overflows from the city's overtaxed drainage system and pollutes the water, making it almost perpetually murky.

Fruge said that before they reached the bridge, Gaede pulled over in an alley and pulled out a gun. He slipped on a pair of gloves purchased at the Fleet Farm back in Fargo. Methodically, he cleaned the weapon, a .32 caliber pistol. Instead of putting the gun back together when he was finished, he left it in three pieces and handed them to his wife.

Gaede drove to the Hoan Bridge and pulled over in the darkness at three separate spots. Each time, Fruge got out of the car and walked to the rail, flinging a piece of the weapon as far as she could into the water.

Gaede then fixated on getting out of Wisconsin and was adamant that once they left, they could never return. The police would be on the lookout for the blue Buick and for every other vehicle associated with Gaede, Fruge or Wicks. They needed some new wheels, and that would cost money. Gaede stopped at several different branches of the

M&I Bank. By the time he'd finished his banking rounds, he was flush with close to $17,000 in cash.

Gaede and Fruge went shopping for a mobile home on Saturday, January 12, 2002. They found a suitable vehicle at Advance Camping Sales in the Milwaukee suburb of Greenfield. It was a 23-foot Travel Master, used most recently by a marching band. After talking about the purchase over lunch, the couple returned to the dealership and paid for their new camper in cash. They were supposed to pick it up the following Monday but were delayed until Tuesday because of some paperwork problems at the dealership.

Then it was back to the Park Motel, where they packed up all their possessions and Wicks' drums. They were in their motel room when Hales Corners Police Officer Pawlak called Gaede's cell phone, looking for Wicks. Gaede stayed cool as he explained to the officer that he was Dennis Johnson from Bismarck and he'd never heard of Wicks. Then he quickly hung up.

Gaede headed to a book store for books on Canada and plenty of maps. He insisted that Fruge drive the camper and meet him later. She'd always driven compact cars, so maneuvering a 23-foot camper out of a motel parking lot was a challenge. When she looked in the rear view mirror, the only thing she saw was Wicks' drum set. Then she saw a squad car.

"God, how am I going to get out of this parking lot?" she muttered to herself. Fruge pulled the massive vehicle onto the street and was amazed when the police car didn't follow.

The couple reunited at Fruge's ex-husband's house in Milwaukee so Joshua could visit with Raychel. When they left, Fruge told her daughter they were headed back to Fargo because Gaede had a job interview the following morning.

In reality, they headed for Canada. As they neared the border, Fruge said, Gaede told her to drive their new RV across. He would walk through the woods, since he'd been banned from the country at the time of his deportation. She should pick him up on the other side.

"We can't do that," Fruge told him. She had taken Joshua from his father. If she tried to take the little boy across the border, surely they would be caught.

They turned around, heading south toward Mexico. They would live on the beach and sell fruit from the back of a truck, Gaede told Fruge, or they could set up a gyros stand. Surely the Mexicans would love a little exotic Greek cuisine. The more Gaede talked about that idea, the more excited he got. He would wear a collar, he told her, like a minister, and tell customers the profits from the gyros supported his church. "Even a padre needs to make a living, hey?" he asked. Fruge agreed it sounded nice, though she was starting to realize it would never happen.

They took turns driving. Joshua sat in a swivel chair in back watching movies on a little TV/VCR combo they'd bought for him. When they stopped, if it was warm enough, Fruge would take her son outside to play, trying to cram a lifetime of parenting into each day, just in case. Before, her biggest concern for Joshua had been his asthma. That seemed like such a small thing now.

Gaede really wanted to keep Wicks' drum set, which was top of the line. But by the time they reached Nashville, they were running out of money. A music shop there had a sign in the window offering new and used instruments for sale. Gaede correctly guessed they would also buy instruments. For the complete set, Zildjian cymbals and all, the couple got $600.

At every campground, Gaede booted up his laptop computer, obsessively scanning web sites to try to stay ahead of the authorities. The news was breaking fast. When the body was found, Gaede knew almost immediately. When the head turned up, he read about it in the news reports. When the body was identified as Wicks, tensions in the camper mounted.

Fruge could no longer bring Joshua outside to play. Gaede wouldn't allow it since boy's picture would be everywhere. The child grew restless, and once Gaede whacked him on the rear end for misbehaving.

"Dennis, I can't do this anymore," Fruge pleaded. "How long can I keep a 3-year-old cooped up in an RV? I just can't live like this anymore." She was sobbing.

"Well, I think we should turn ourselves in," he said, surprising her.

But first, there was something he needed her to do.

*　　　　*　　　　*

On February 7, Gaede's sister, Sue Coons, called the Hales Corners Police Department with a tip. She suspected her brother was at their mother's house. Coons had gone to Hazel's to look for some gloves that one of her children might have left there. Hazel refused to let Coons into the house, saying she would look for the gloves herself. Coons asked if she could come in and have something to eat.

"I haven't got any food in the house," Hazel said.

Coons' suspicions grew. She knew her mother had just bought a bunch of pork chops. There was no way she'd eaten them all.

As Hazel looked for the gloves, Coons went to the back yard. There were piles of trash, including fried chicken boxes. Fried chicken was Gaede's favorite food. She noticed the second-floor drapes were closed. Hazel usually kept them open during the day.

"When was the last time you saw Dennis?" Coons asked.

"It's been a while," Hazel answered.

"Aren't you worried about him?" Coons pressed.

"No," her mother replied. "I know he hasn't done anything wrong."

After Schoonover heard about Coons' call, he contacted the Milwaukee County district attorney's office in hopes of getting a search warrant. An assistant prosecutor told Schoonover some closed drapes and empty chicken boxes weren't enough to establish probable cause. Schoonover wished he could stake out the house himself, but he had no jurisdiction in Milwaukee.

Instead, he called Milwaukee's District Seven police station and informed the district commander that a murder suspect might be in their area. Schoonover faxed over photos of Gaede and the mobile home, as well as the APB out of Michigan and the press release the Michigan State Police had sent out when they found Wicks' head.

Schoonover had a hunch Gaede's sister's suspicions were justified. He could only hope his fellow officers would somehow lay eyes on Gaede and arrest him.

The next day, February 8, Fruge was scheduled for yet another custody hearing to argue with Barranco about visitation for Joshua. Fruge didn't want to miss the court appearance. She knew that if she didn't show up, her son could end up with his father for good.

"Just call and tell them you hurt your back. They'll have to reschedule it," Gaede urged.

"No," she said. "If you want to lie like that, you do it."

So he did. It was obvious to Fruge that no one would believe him, but Gaede didn't seem concerned.

After the hearing, Gaede called Fruge's lawyer, Shauntelle VanBeek.

"How did the hearing go?" he asked, cool, calm and collected. Listening to only Gaede's side of the conversation, it was obvious to Fruge that her lawyer knew something was suspicious. After a few minutes, Gaede ended the call by saying: "She can't talk right now. I'm on a pay phone." Then he hung up.

VanBeek hit *69 and wrote down the Chicago telephone number that came up. She called the Hales Corners police to relay the information. A few minutes later, Fruge called the attorney herself.

"Diane, you need to go to the nearest police department and turn yourself in," VanBeek told her client.

"Why?" Fruge asked.

"If you ever want to see your child again, you need to turn yourself in," VanBeek answered.

"Why?" Fruge asked again.

"Your husband is wanted for murder," VanBeek replied, telling Fruge something she was sure Fruge already knew.

"Murder? What?"

VanBeek tried again. "Where are you?"

"We're in Fargo," Fruge answered, then continued with the lie her husband had concocted. "I fell down the basement stairs and I really hurt my back. I couldn't make it to Milwaukee."

VanBeek made no progress with Fruge, who soon hung up. This time, when VanBeek hit *69, it came back "number unknown."

*   *   *

Camp-A-Way, a private campground in Lincoln, Nebraska, was one of the nicest Fruge and Gaede had visited on their cross-country journey. There were clean showers and a laundry room. Fruge begged Gaede to stay one more day so she could wash Joshua's sheets and blankets. Joshua had been wetting the bed lately, his mother guessed from nerves.

Gaede relented. It was just the break the authorities needed. As the family settled in for a second night in Lincoln, television news broadcasts in North Dakota flashed footage from a news conference earlier in the day. An FBI agent said Gaede was wanted for questioning in a killing and described him as armed and dangerous.

An anonymous tipster who called himself Duane Strute and his wife had recently returned from their camping trip to Nashville. Strute was watching television that night at their home in the Red River Valley in Minnesota, just across the state line from Fargo. When photos of the suspects flashed on the screen, Strute recognized the little boy whose family had camped next to his back in Tennessee. He called the FBI. The description he gave of their RV was the same as the one Fruge bought back in Wisconsin, right down to the broken orange light on the back.

Agents were immediately dispatched to Nashville, where a campground operator confirmed that Gaede and Fruge had been there. The couple had been on their way to Lincoln, the worker told authorities.

The next afternoon, March 4, 2002, Fruge saw the first police car and wondered for a moment why it was there. Private campgrounds had their own security and didn't usually call in the city police. Before Fruge could complete the thought, more squad cars followed. Maybe 10, maybe a dozen. Cops with guns surrounded them.

"I think we're going down," Fruge told her husband.

She was right.

"Joshua, Mom's going to have to go away for a while," she told her son as the authorities closed in.

"Why, were you bad?"

She bit her lip to keep from crying. "It doesn't mean I'm a bad person, but I did a bad thing. You're going to have to live with your dad for a while."

Her son was sobbing, then screaming.

"Be strong and stay with your dad until Mommy can come and find you," Fruge murmured to the frantic child.

"I'm going out first," Gaede told her. He didn't want Joshua getting shot.

Gaede walked out of the RV with his hands up. Immediately, a bunch of cops took him to the ground and cuffed his hands behind his back. "There's meat on the counter," he tried to tell them. "Put that meat away or it will spoil."

"Shut up," one of the officers replied.

All Gaede could think about was rancid meat. By the time he got out of jail and got back to the RV, it would stink to high heaven. He and Fruge might never get the smell out.

Officers put Gaede into the back seat of a squad car. Meanwhile, they were shouting for Fruge to come out with her hands up.

Joshua was attached to her leg. Fruge walked as best she could, holding him with one hand as she raised the other into the air.

"Do you have any weapons?" one of the cops asked her.

"No. No," she replied.

The cops didn't try to separate the boy from her as they took her into custody. The officers patted down both mother and child, then led them to another squad car for the drive to the jail in Lancaster County, Nebraska. There, Fruge would be booked on a Wisconsin charge of interfering with child custody. When she missed her earlier court date, she had committed a felony. Joshua would be put into the custody of child protective services until Barranco could pick him up.

Fruge was in tears as she entered the booking area at the Lancaster County Jail. Once she was photographed and fingerprinted, she was led to a holding cell. The booking officers wanted Fruge evaluated before they moved her to more permanent lodging.

The woman called in to do the job was Correctional Specialist Sherri Cotter. Cotter had worked in corrections for 15 years. Her primary responsibility was evaluating inmates' mental health. If the officers at the booking desk had concerns about a new prisoner, they called Cotter. She determined whether people like Fruge should be housed

102

with the general population, in solitary confinement, or on suicide watch. Cotter continued to monitor inmates after booking to make sure their mental health didn't decline in jail.

Cotter wanted to be sure Fruge was aware of all the publicity about Wicks' death so she would be prepared for the other inmates' reactions. Cotter introduced herself, making it clear that she was not there to discuss the details of Fruge's case or to interrogate her in any way. Cotter handed Fruge a copy of the March 6 edition of the *Lincoln Journal Star*. The newspaper detailed the arrest scene at the Lincoln campground. It said Gaede was wanted for questioning in the grizzly murder of Wicks and described the dismembered corpse.

Fruge read the article, and then burst into tears. "I'm never going to be able to face my family again," she sobbed. "Dennis didn't do this. I did it."

CHAPTER TWELVE

Fruge's outburst at the Lancaster County Jail wasn't the first time she had confessed to killing Timothy Wicks.

Attorney Bridget Boyle had represented Gaede during his trial in Monroe County, as well as helping him out of some of his other minor scrapes around the state. The attorney's pixie haircut belied the forceful manner she had inherited from her father and law partner, Jerry Boyle.

The elder Boyle was legendary in Milwaukee. He reveled in publicity and was one of a handful of Milwaukee lawyers who faithfully returned reporters' calls, passing out his cell phone number to anyone who wanted it. Jerry Boyle had represented Jeffrey Dahmer, the infamous serial killer who had haunted Milwaukee between 1987 and 1991. Boyle became a regular commentator on Court TV after that.

Although Bridget Boyle had decades less experience than her father, by 2002 she had gained a reputation of her own. Gaede was smitten with her. He was certain she could help him and his wife out of the Wicks mess.

According to Gaede and Fruge, they were on the road in the RV when Fruge called Bridget Boyle and confessed both the killing and the dismemberment. "I killed him in self-defense," Fruge told Boyle. "He tried to rape me."

"I'm afraid I can't help you," Fruge recalled Boyle saying. "It wouldn't be right, since I've represented Dennis." The attorney urged the couple to turn themselves in. If they did, Boyle said, she would find another attorney to assist them.

Around the time she called Boyle, a few days before the authorities closed in, Fruge also had written a confession. She sat down in the RV and wrote a paragraph or two, detailing a rape attempt by Wicks that ended with her fatally shooting him. The last time Fruge saw the written confession, it was in Gaede's day planner, which was inside the RV. By the time Fruge arrived at the Lancaster County Jail, she assumed the FBI had it.

According to Gaede, the rape attempt was a horrible end to a friendship that became a business relationship and then spun out of control. It all started back in 2000, around the time he met Fruge. Gaede was running two profitable businesses, Lodis Financial Group and Hudson Bay Bait and Tackle, in West Allis, Wisconsin. Wicks, Gaede said, was his partner in those businesses. As it turned out, Wicks had training in accounting, Gaede said. Gaede gave him a few tips, and he could do tax work just fine.

After Gaede was convicted of the charges of escape and aiding a felon in Monroe County, he came back to their suburban Milwaukee office panicked, he said.

"I can't go to prison," he said desperately.

"What can we do to help?" a co-worker asked.

Gaede thought back to his days in Canada and asked, half-joking, "Anybody got an ID I can borrow?"

Wicks volunteered his, Gaede said. Wicks handed over an extra driver's license and a duplicate Social Security card. He ordered an extra copy of his birth certificate for Gaede. Gaede said he planned to use Wicks' identity only temporarily, then planned to create an entirely new identity out of whole cloth. The only reason he didn't do that in the first place was that he didn't have the time.

Meanwhile, Gaede said, he brought Wicks into a partnership buying North Dakota real estate. Gaede said he bought the farmhouse in Gardner in Wicks' name with Wicks' cooperation, had it re-appraised, and learned that he could sell it for $28,000 more than they had paid. A few months before he died, Wicks visited Fargo, and the two of them checked out two more houses in the North Dakota towns of Enderlin and South Heart. The real estate agent didn't come along, but simply gave them the codes for the key boxes on the vacant homes, Gaede said.

Gaede said he didn't know if Wicks ever attacked Fruge. He said he did know there were problems between the two, though. Fruge felt threatened when her new house was purchased in Wicks' name. She and her first husband had lost their first house to foreclosure, and she was determined not to lose another one, Gaede said.

The plan to go to Canada with Wicks grew out of the two men's mutual love of performing, Gaede said. From his past life in Winnipeg, Gaede knew the music scene there was fantastic. Gaede could find a gig most every night, either solo, with his band, or at an open-mike night. He said he never promised Wicks a specific deal at any one bar. Instead, Wicks planned to move to the border between North Dakota and Canada so the two of them could travel north and check out the scene whenever the mood struck them. Gaede and Fruge went to Wisconsin to pick up their friend shortly after Christmas 2001, Gaede said.

On the drive back to North Dakota, Gaede said, he and Wicks were in separate cars. They feared being pulled over and being forced to present drivers' licenses in the same name. Wicks also feared getting lost, so Fruge hopped into his Cavalier. Gaede, meanwhile, packed his Buick full of their belongings from Wisconsin to take to their new house. They would not travel in tandem. Rather, each vehicle would leave at a different time and travel a different route. Gaede said he left first, and he doesn't know what became of his friend and his wife after that.

Days later, on December 27, Gaede still had not seen his wife, although he said she called a couple of times. He went to work. When he returned, Wicks' car was in the driveway, but the house was dark. Wicks wasn't there, and neither was Fruge.

She called him often in the next few days, sobbing and hysterical, he said. She wouldn't tell him where she was. Gaede figured Fruge had gone back to Wisconsin and something bad had happened with Barranco. He figured she

107

would tell him about it once she sobered up and calmed down.

When Fruge finally showed up back in Gardner three days later, Gaede asked her what had become of Wicks.

"The guys from Winnipeg picked him up already," she said.

Gaede said he didn't doubt the story. About a week later, they returned to Wisconsin to drop off Joshua for a visit with his dad. As they drove through Milwaukee's suburbs, Gaede mused, "I wonder how Tim's doing."

He said his wife looked at him guiltily, saying, "I've got something to tell you." He braced for the worst, expecting his wife to tell him she'd slept with his friend. Instead, she confessed to killing him.

"I almost crashed the car," Gaede said.

He said he agreed to go on the run to protect his beloved wife, and to keep Joshua away from Barranco. But if they were caught, he told her, she needed to come clean.

*   *   *

After they were arrested at the RV park, both Fruge and Gaede refused to waive extradition. They sat in jail in Nebraska, Fruge on the custody charge and Gaede in connection with the embezzlement from Compressed Air. Gaede's bail was $3 million cash. Fruge's was $1 million. If jail hadn't been so depressing, Fruge would have laughed. Fruge considered herself the least dangerous person on earth. She didn't even kill bugs. Raychel, at 12, had beaten up her mother without much trouble.

The high bail amounts reinforced something Gaede and Fruge both knew. It was only a matter of time before one or both of them was charged with something a lot more serious in connection with Wicks' death.

Cass County Sheriff's Lt. Majerus immediately left Fargo for Nebraska, but it was a wasted trip. Both suspects had asked for lawyers immediately, and both lawyers had advised their clients not to talk.

Meanwhile, Cotter had decided Fruge was mentally stable and could be lodged with the general population. Fruge was assigned to share a cell with a huge lesbian nicknamed Biggie. They got along fine, except when Fruge's bouts of insomnia disrupted Biggie's sleep. Then they would argue, and Biggie would hold a grudge until Fruge sneaked her a contraband candy bar. Fruge did her best to avoid candy, but sticking to a low-calorie diet was impossible, considering the jail cuisine. Between that and the prohibition on smoking, she feared her weight would creep back up to its pre-stomach stapling levels.

Fruge put her beauty school training to use and started doing haircuts for the other girls on the cell block. She created makeshift makeup for them and herself using pencils, pens, emery boards, toothpaste and butter from breakfast. She also tended to mother the younger girls, reminding them to say "please" and "thank you."

During her first two weeks in jail, Fruge suspected she might be pregnant. She was both relived and slightly sad when she realized it was a false alarm. She would have loved to have a baby with Gaede, but not if they had to stay in jail while their child was raised by strangers.

Meanwhile, when Gaede's fellow inmates learned the details of his alleged crime, they immediately dubbed him "cool," he said. Several different gangs tried to recruit him. For a time, Gaede was kept in protective custody behind Plexiglas. He was surprised they didn't post some kind of sign: "Danger. Keep away from the glass." The gang bangers gazed at Gaede with respect when they passed by, he said, throwing up hand signs in hopes that he would return them. He didn't. Instead, he waited eagerly for his visits from the chaplain and spent most of his time on Bible lessons.

For both Fruge and Gaede, there was one bright spot in their incarcerations. When someone opened the door between the male and female sides of the jail, or if they loitered at a window at just the right moment, they could catch glimpses of each other. Even though they were in the same building, their sole means of communication was the mail. Fruge got a letter from her husband almost immediately after they were arrested.

Dear my sweet love Diane,

It breaks my heart to see you locked up suffering in that small cell. Every time I heard keys gingle (sic) or a door open I jumped up to see if I could get a short glimpse of you. No torture could even measure the pain of knowing you were twenty feet away and that I couldn't touché (sic) or see you. Sometimes I would hear you crying and I would start too.

As time went on, Gaede was more prone to start his letters with a simple "Hi Sweetheart." The letters were filled with details of his days in jail, legal advice about the theory of self-defense and desperate expressions of his love and devotion.

I need you in my life so bad, sweetheart, it just hurts. I'm so happy that I fell in love with you. This was the best year of my life. Please stay in touch with me, I really need to hear from you. I love you very much.

For Fruge, sometimes her husband's letters were comforting, but sometimes they made her cry. When Gaede mentioned calling Judy, an old girlfriend of his in Canada, for information about how the story was playing out in the media up there, Fruge's heart nearly broke, and she burst into tears.

The next letter she received from her husband didn't do much to ease her emotional state.

I hope you realize how much money I am going to sue these bastards for when this is over. By her (Judy) telling me I was all across Canada on the TV news and paper, that means that I went international. With your statement that is defamation of character. They've killed me in the media with no evidence. I spoke to a lawyer already and he said he would start a 50 million yes 50 million dollar law-suit against the FBI or federal government for damages starting with slander.

The letter she received two days later wasn't any better.

The good news is that I spent all morning at the law library researching self defense issues. I would bet that you are going to win. ...

If one through an honest conviction induced by reasonable evidence that he is in imminent danger of receiving great bodily harm, takes the life of another, he will NOT be held responsible criminally, although (maybe/maybe not) mistaken as to the extent of the actual danger, if other responsible and judicious men would have been alike mistaken.

Read that statement a thousand times until you understand it 100%. This is YOU!!! You need women jurors for this one, hopefully a few battered wives. It's just like the other one that I sent you about the battered one from that book. It fits like a glove. Another statute said that you can use such means for self protection if you are violently assaulted!! The key is that you must have tried all reasonable means to escape without killing. Neither front doors worked right — they stick, no phone, only door was the back door.

The max that you would do is 5 years, 60 months, with good time 40 months or 3 years, 4 months. I think that that is the max I can get in Wisconsin too. Prisons are way overcrowded and you have no record and mine isn't that bad all misdemeanors up until now. You might not do any time. Nothing would make me happier than to see you walk away from this clean.

... I had a dream about you last night. We were at a park and some bees were flying around so I stepped on them. We saw a couple more and decided to leave. You were grabbing the blanket and stuff but you couldn't carry everything. You left my briefcase and went back to get it.

Just then I noticed about a million bees swarming above a tree nearby. I got in the car and started the motor and as you came up to the back of the car the bees attacked you. You threw the blanket over yourself and got down on the ground. I hesitated and didn't get out of the car because I knew that they would kill me but I wanted to save you. I got so upset that I woke up.

The point is that the time came for me to give my life for you and I hesitated then woke up and I know that I would have. I feel like such a coward because I know you'd do it for me. You proved it to me.

I feel like I just can't live with myself over what you're doing. ...

I still cry every day because of you. Nothing ever hurt me like this sweetheart. I love you so much. And everybody thinks I'm this big tough guy. I can be at times but never with you. I'm going to close this letter from the deepest depths of my heart.

Forever & ever, Dennis

As was his custom in his letters to his wife, Gaede had coated his lips with Blistex and kissed the paper beside his signature.

Along with professions of her love, most of Fruge's letters to her husband included graphic sexual fantasies. The letters also usually included slice-of-life tales.

They pick on me sometimes about the newspaper article. I just tell people, "I'm only here on a (sic) interference with custody charge. But still I've heard, "Hey, Sher, why don't you give Diane a hand?" or some people will be arguing and this smart ass Cindy says "Well don't chop my head off — no offense Diane." These people are real lucky I have a sense of humor.

On March 21, Fruge wrote to Gaede about her first meeting with her public defender.

Well, I just had a contact visit with my lawyer. I had to destroy my statement. He said that statement would bury me, too much time span after the rape when he got in the shower — said I had time to get out of the house without the rest ... you know. He said that with a statement like that in Nebraska I'd end up with the death penalty or minimum of life. When you get extradited, you are going to have to make a statement against me.

Gaede immediately wrote back, telling about a conversation he'd had with his sister, Sue Coons.

I just talked to Susie and she said that the police got a search warrant for my house in Michigan. She said that they have been there several times and took some items. She also said that I'm the only one that's on the news and it's getting hot. Please help me. If the cops have been there that many times they must think that they have something. I'm in enough shit that I don't need this too. If someone tells them that I had nothing to do with it, it will stop them in their tracks. Especially if there was a full confession to the crime. They're slamming me so bad honey that they're going to hang me on everything.

Babe, I just got your letter from Thursday where you said you were ripping up the statement. I don't know what the time line was, but take in account that you were scared because of the warrants out on me, being fucked up, getting dressed and looking for your cell phone can take some time. Plus you said that Josh woke up because you were crying and you had to put him back to sleep, I think. Regardless of how it happened, it did.

I don't know if I can make a statement against you. Please don't be mad but I think if they charge me I'm going to my original plan that clears you completely. Please don't tell anyone what my plan is because I want this to be my choice and not someone else's.

Days later, he wrote again, desperate.

I just have to figure out a new game plan. Just fix the time line. ... Just remember that the song remains the same just change the timing in it. Draw a line on a piece of paper. Mark the hours of a clock on it. Fill in the gaps and look for the holes. Be prepared for questions about that *orange truck. I have a feeling they will come up. ... If they think that you're helping me, please convince them that you're not. And also don't forget that I quit Comp Air on the 29th because of Jeff saying I never worked a full week since I started. ... Remember something else, if there was no <u>intent</u> it wasn't premeditated and therefore it's <u>a lot</u> less. Like you said you need a good defense lawyer.*

For weeks, both Fruge and Gaede continued to refuse to waive extradition. Then Fruge's public defender informed her that sitting in jail in Nebraska was essentially a waste of time. If she was convicted and sentenced to jail or prison time in Wisconsin or North Dakota, those states wouldn't give her credit for the time she served in Nebraska. When that sank in, Fruge decided she would be better off going to Wisconsin to deal with the child custody charge.

Shortly after Fruge left Lincoln, Gaede decided there was no point in continuing to sit there. He couldn't glimpse his wife through the doorways anymore or pass notes across to her in the women's wing. Gaede refused to return to Wisconsin, though. He was sure the bikers and crooked cops there would kill him if he showed up in a prison in his home state. He was allowed to go to North Dakota instead.

Neither Gaede nor Fruge was charged with homicide, but almost as soon as Gaede arrived in Fargo, he realized there was no getting away from his former enemies. According to Gaede, one of the first guys who approached him in the cell block was clearly a biker, a member of the Hell's Angels.

"Your friends from Winnipeg said to tell you hi," the guy said, full of menace.

Gaede knew it was a threat, but he wouldn't back down. Later, he wrote to Fruge:

They offered me a membership just to keep me quiet about some things that I know about. It clearly was a threat. Well, anyway, two other people heard it and they

114

told the guards about it. Now the police believe what I've been telling them all along. Anyway, the guy got put in segregation because of it. Now the police really want to talk to me! I'm scheduled to talk to the DA and the US attorney general next week about all of this shit. If they ask about T.W. I can't tell them anything because I don't know anything.

Of course, when Gaede met with the FBI and Majerus of the Cass County Sheriff's Department, Tim Wicks was all they wanted to hear about. Gaede came up with explanations for many of his actions, saying he had rented the backhoe to fix his foundation problems, and he had rented the U-Haul to move a wood stove from his cabin in Michigan.

The cops asked repeatedly why he would drive the truck all the way to Michigan from South Dakota. Why not just rent it in Michigan? They didn't seem satisfied with his answers, and when he tried to tell them the bikers were setting him up, they didn't listen.

Shortly thereafter, the jail psychiatrist put Gaede on medication. His anxiety at the thought of imprisonment in Wisconsin was enough to make him suicidal.

I can beat most of the charges here, he wrote Fruge from North Dakota, *but then I take my chances in Wisconsin. After the threat that I got here I really don't want to go to prison in Wisconsin. I want you to know that I wasn't kidding when I told you that I was set up on charges so they could kill me. ... I don't like feeling threatened and I do right now.*

It didn't take long for word of Fruge's confession to make its way from the Lancaster County Jail in Nebraska back to Detective Schoonover in Wisconsin. It should have been a satisfying moment in his career, the moment he solved one of the most gruesome murders he'd ever encountered. There was just one problem. Schoonover's gut told him Fruge was lying. He didn't know why. He didn't know if he could ever prove it. But his gut was almost never wrong.

CHAPTER THIRTEEN

Cass County State's Attorney Birch Burdick's roots were firmly planted in the soil of North Dakota. His grandfather, Usher L. Burdick, was a United States Congressman, as was his father, Quentin Northrup Burdick. Quentin Burdick served for just under two years in the U.S. House of Representatives, then went on to serve as a senator for more than 30 years, from 1960 until his death in 1992. Quentin Burdick died in the middle of his term, so Birch's mother, Jocelyn Birch Burdick, was appointed to serve until a special election could be held.

At first, the couple's son avoided politics. Birch Burdick graduated from Fargo South High School in 1973. He left home and turned an aptitude for math into an engineering degree from the University of Michigan. For 11 years, he worked as a nuclear and mechanical engineer, designing and operating nuclear power plants for electric companies. His engineering career led him around the country and the world.

Eventually, Burdick decided he wanted to return home, but there wasn't much demand for nuclear engineers in North Dakota. He figured law would be an interesting and challenging career back in the Midwest. Despite his attorney father's advice that the move was ill-advised considering his successful engineering career, Burdick applied for law school. Shortly after arriving at the University of Minnesota's Hamline School of Law, he stuffed his television set in the closet because it distracted him from his studies. He graduated in 1992, the same year his famous father died, and went into private practice, becoming part of the family legacy that included at least four attorneys in the two generations before him. A mere six years later, he defeated one of his high school classmates in the Cass County state's attorney's race and had served ever since.

Around the time of Gaede's arrest, Burdick took an interest in playing the electric guitar. He admitted that although he'd bought the instrument and went to all the lessons, he never practiced, so he wasn't any good.

In legal circles, Burdick was known for his integrity, intelligence and common sense. He felt that as a prosecutor, he made a positive contribution to the community. Like many elected prosecutors, however, he didn't spend the majority of his time in the courtroom. During one of his re-election campaigns, his opponent ran on the platform that unlike Burdick, he would actually try cases. Nonetheless, Burdick won the election. He continued to try a few cases himself, but remained willing to let capable assistants handle many of the courtroom appearances.

Burdick was in no rush to issue murder charges against either Gaede or Fruge. Gaede seemed the more likely culprit, yet Fruge had confessed, and her husband backed up her story. The prosecutor didn't want to make the wrong choice.

Burdick first assigned Gaede's case to a junior assistant, Jennifer Thompson, who worked property crimes. It was her responsibility to deal with Compressed Air's missing money. She charged Gaede with three felonies. When Gaede's attorney argued for bail, Thompson told the judge Gaede was a suspect in a possible homicide. Even if he made bail in North Dakota, he would be on his way to jail in Wisconsin, she said. Over Thompson's objection, the judge set Gaede's bail at $100,000. He didn't post it.

The plea negotiations began. Threatened with being sent back to Wisconsin, Gaede readily admitted insurance fraud. He'd applied for health insurance and received benefits under the name Tim Wicks. He wasn't Tim Wicks. That was plainly fraud, and he was sorry. He also agreed to plead guilty to theft, even though he said he hadn't technically stolen anything, he just took loans from the business accounts and didn't pay the money back quickly enough.

A charge of identity theft, though, was a major sticking point. There was no way he was pleading guilty to that. Gaede insisted he hadn't stolen Wicks' identity.

Rather, his friend had been helping him out by allowing the ruse, plain and simple.

In the end, Thompson was willing to change the identity theft charge to "theft by deception" in order to get Gaede to plead guilty. Both crimes covered the essential facts of the case, and both were felonies. To Thompson, it was all semantics. It didn't matter what you called it, Gaede would do serious time. He was convicted of all three crimes in August 2002 and sentenced to four years in prison.

In Thompson's view, Gaede was smarter than the average criminal. She didn't believe for a second that Wicks had agreed to give up his identity. She thought Gaede had very carefully planned out his move to North Dakota and his new life as Tim Wicks. From what she could tell, his assimilation into small-town North Dakota had been pretty easy.

Gardner was the perfect place for such a scheme. People there, as in all of North Dakota, were very trusting. The small town boasted a friendly, open atmosphere, where people expected the best of their neighbors. People also kept an eye on their neighbors. That was the only thing that led Thompson to believe maybe the blue farmhouse wasn't a crime scene. No one had reported any strange activity there. No witnesses had come forward. If someone had seen or heard anything, word would have spread quickly.

After Gaede's sentencing for the crimes at Compressed Air, a reporter asked Burdick if there were any other charges pending against Gaede. Burdick said no. People inside Burdick's office knew that wasn't entirely true. Thompson, with an embezzlement conviction, had gotten Gaede locked up for several years. As a result, her boss and his colleagues in two other states had time to figure out what to do about the homicide without worrying that their suspect was walking the streets or disappearing to Canada.

There was a jurisdictional problem with the murder charges. No one was sure that the crime had taken place in

119

North Dakota. That was the most basic fact needed before Burdick could charge the case. With no physical evidence, there was no easy way to figure out whether the murder scene was in North Dakota, Michigan or Wisconsin. Everyone involved in the investigation would have loved to see Gaede confess to killing Wicks, but Thompson didn't think it was likely. From what she could tell, it wasn't in Gaede's personality. The most accurate word the assistant prosecutor could come up with to describe her suspect was "smooth." Take his first court appearance in the embezzlement case. By the time he got to court, the media had already reported the discovery of Wicks' body, and Gaede knew it. Yet as he stood before the judge, he was calm and not at all animated. It wasn't the demeanor Thompson had come to expect from someone who had committed a serious crime.

Thompson figured Gaede was a habitual liar. He'd rehearsed his story so many times, he probably believed it himself. She knew that if it came down to murder charges, she wouldn't be on the case, and that was okay with her. She knew it wouldn't be an easy case to win, particularly if Gaede got on the stand. She wouldn't want to cross-examine him. The jurors would be waiting for him to crack, the way defendants always did on television, and Thompson was certain Gaede wouldn't. He was a master of deception.

As you probably heard, I got sentenced to four years in prison, Gaede wrote Fruge after the embezzlement case was concluded. *But I should be out within a year from now because the crime was not violent and I have 229 days in already. I qualify for parole even before I get to prison. I'm still here at the jail because the police and the FBI are questioning me about the Wicks deal so they haven't sent me to (prison in) Bismarck yet. ... I am sure that they will be coming to talk to you too. Be prepared and ask for a lawyer before anything.*

FBI Special Agent John Dalziel interviewed Gaede without a lawyer three times before the prisoner headed for Bismarck. The first time, Dalziel was assisted by Fargo Investigator Tammy Lynk. During the other two interviews, Lt. Rick Majerus of the Cass County Sheriff's Department accompanied Dalziel.

Gaede was more than happy to talk about his past life in Wisconsin, his time in Canada and what he claimed was the corruption at Compressed Air. But every time the officers asked him about Wicks, he changed the subject and clammed up.

"I didn't steal that identity," he said during the first interview.

"Timothy gave it to you?" Dalziel asked.

"Yes."

"When did you meet Tim?" the FBI agent continued.

"In the winter of 2001, you know, tax season, January or February, 2001. He came to me with a problem with the IRS and asked me if I could fix it and I said yes. It was all about tax evasion. He was falsifying tax returns for quite some time. I refused to file a false return. That's the same thing that happened with Compressed Air. I refused to file a false return for them."

Then he was off, going on about Compressed Air for what seemed like hours.

"Did Timothy know you bought the house?" Dalziel asked eventually.

"Yes."

"Did he know you had a bank account in his name?" the FBI agent asked.

"Check the phone records," Gaede instructed. "We were in constant contact. Tim was my good friend."

Before he would discuss Wicks further, Gaede told Dalziel and Lynk that he needed immunity from prosecution, not on the murder charges, but on something else.

"All this will make sense," he promised. "My lawyer has evidence, hard copy evidence that will corroborate. It's going to tell you that what I'm telling you is the truth. It's going to show you that you're looking in the wrong direction."

Later he implicated Fruge, telling the police they needed to hear about a story she had told a lawyer and a priest. He suspected she must have had help, either from Barranco or from a masculine-looking woman in a red pickup truck whom Gaede believed was Fruge's lesbian lover.

"There's a lot of cops that know me. They'll tell you that I'm not a fucking idiot and I'm not somebody that would do this," he insisted. "I mean, I'm still a licensed paramedic. You think with as many lives as I tried to save that I would take somebody's? This is stupid. I understand that you're trying to do your job, but you're looking at the wrong person. ... There is no way I would do something so stupid."

Gaede described his wife as a "Jekyll and Hyde" type and told the police she planned to kill Barranco when she got out of jail.

"Was Timothy sexually abusing Diana? Did he rape her? Is that the piece that we're missing?" Dalziel asked. Gaede hedged, and again asked for immunity. "Number one: You've got a signed confession from Diana, do you not?" he finally asked the FBI agent.

Dalziel and Lynk shook their heads, and Gaede looked stunned.

"I have no signed confession, Dennis," Dalziel said. "No bullshit. And I have everything. I am the case agent. I have all the evidence."

The FBI had searched the entire RV, including Gaede's day planner. The confession, in a sealed envelope, had been inside, Gaede was sure. Yet the police had found nothing.

By the end of the interview, Dalziel and Lynk had planted a seed. Was it possible that Fruge had changed her mind, destroyed the confession, and tried to set up her husband to take the fall instead?

During the second interview, about a week later, Dalziel and Majerus tried to pin down Gaede on specific dates and times. Gaede continued to try and put the blame on Fruge. In the process, he made several admissions that fit with their theory that he was the guilty one, not his wife. He admitted renting the backhoe, but said he needed it to excavate his basement. He admitted renting the U-Haul, saying he drove it to Michigan to get a wood-burning stove to heat his basement. Yet when he and Fruge arrived at the cabin in Powers, she was too drunk to help him lug it out of the house, so they left. He admitted buying supplies at Fleet Farm, including boots, a hatchet and a pruning saw, but said he planned to use them to set up the stove when he got it back to Gardner.

During the third and final interview, Gaede turned over the letters Fruge had written him from jail. He pointed out several parts he thought the police would find interesting, including a section in which Fruge said Gaede would probably have to make a statement against her in order for her to be sent back to Fargo.

"Why would she be so willing for you to incriminate her?" Majerus asked.

Gaede thought for a minute, then answered, "We have a relationship where I would never let her take the blame for something I did, and she would never let me take the blame for something she did. And she knew damn well that I was going to be the target of this because of the circumstances. ... In all the time that I've been here, it never even crossed my mind that I could have been set up on this until you said that the other day."

Majerus and Dalziel cut the final interview far shorter than the first two. They were getting nowhere.

Meanwhile, Schoonover and Milwaukee County District Attorney E. Michael McCann were considering an alternative plan, in case a murder prosecution proved impossible. A federal kidnapping charge was problematic, since Wicks had told virtually everyone he knew that he was going to Canada voluntarily. If authorities in Wisconsin and Michigan made a case for dismemberment or mutilating a corpse, it would be tough to prove without physical evidence. Milwaukee County's only option was a forgery charge, based on the fact that Gaede had cleared out Wicks' Milwaukee bank accounts. Bank surveillance video clearly showed Gaede making the withdrawals, and the signature on the withdrawal slip matched the one on Gaede's North Dakota driver's license — the one with Wicks' name and Gaede's picture.

Assistant District Attorney DeAnn Heard filed the forgery charge. It would be waiting if Gaede ever got out of prison in North Dakota.

CHAPTER FOURTEEN

Despite her husband's attempts to implicate her, Fruge wasn't charged with anything in North Dakota or Nebraska and was sent back to Wisconsin. Schoonover saw Fruge's return to Milwaukee as a golden opportunity to interview her and get at the truth. The charge of interfering with child custody was a law enforcement strategy to compel her return to Wisconsin and then gain her cooperation. Schoonover hoped the felony charge would be enough to motivate Fruge to tell what she knew about Wicks' murder. Schoonover believed she would agree to help them catch Gaede, the real killer. In return, the child custody charge would disappear.

But Fruge didn't cooperate in the way Schoonover had hoped. At her first court appearance on the felony charge, on April 17, 2002, Assistant District Attorney Carole Crowley called Fruge "a very serious flight risk."

"She obviously was in Nebraska," Crowley told Milwaukee County Court Commissioner Barry C. Seagle. "She's been on the run since January, and there are allegations that she and her husband are involved in other criminal activity as well. He's also in Nebraska or North Dakota and is now facing charges in both states."

Crowley couldn't discuss Wicks' murder in detail since no charges had been issued, but she was well aware of the investigation. Her job was to make sure Fruge didn't make bail and disappear again.

Seagle set bail at $100,000 cash, which Fruge had no hope of posting, even with her mother's help. Fruge was sent back to the Milwaukee County House of Correction, a facility that housed defendants awaiting trial, non-violent people serving short sentences and those eligible for work release.

Fruge's attorney, Craig Johnson, made it clear that he was open to receiving a call from Burdick, but Burdick never called him. Schoonover was eager to talk with Fruge, but the Milwaukee County district attorney wouldn't allow it. If the crime had occurred as Fruge said, following a rape attempt at the Gardner farmhouse, Wisconsin didn't have jurisdiction. So if Schoonover questioned Fruge and got a confession, it could be thrown out of court. As a result, the murder was left out of the plea negotiations.

Fruge had just one conviction on her record, a DUI that dated back to 1997. It was surprising that she didn't have more, since she had struggled with alcoholism for 20 years. One of the false insurance claims Gaede was convicted of making was actually for the in-patient alcohol treatment Fruge had received in Fargo. Nonetheless, entering the program wasn't a crime on Fruge's part. And in Wisconsin, a first-offense DUI wasn't even a misdemeanor. It was a municipal offense, like speeding, and the penalty was a ticket.

Fruge had been arrested one other time, for shoplifting in Florida. A friend of hers had convinced Fruge it would be fun to pocket a bra from a department store. Fruge's friend, a seasoned shoplifter, got away. Fruge was arrested, but the charges were later dropped.

In the end, Fruge foiled Schoonover's strategy by agreeing to plead guilty to the child custody charge. Crowley promised to recommend a long probation term and no additional jail time.

Fruge's sentencing hearing was scheduled for the morning of July 2, 2002, the day Raychel would graduate from eighth grade. With luck, Fruge would be sentenced, processed by the probation department and out of custody in time to attend the afternoon ceremony. Fruge prayed she would make it in time. She felt so guilty for what she had done to Raychel and was desperate to be a mother to her again.

As the sentencing hearing began, defense attorney Johnson told Judge David Hansher that Fruge "absolutely and categorically denies any involvement in the homicide of this person" — meaning Wicks. "The fact that she's obviously married to somebody who is a suspect is something that ... she has no control over," Johnson said.

Then Joshua's father got his turn. "My son is 4," Barranco told the judge in broken English. "He said every time he asked for me, she spank him and slap him in his face. My son have nightmares. They were running from state to state. A lot of things that happen in that trailer."

Fruge could hardly contain her anger. She wanted to tell the judge what a hypocrite Joshua's father was. She'd only taken off with Gaede and Joshua in the first place because Barranco had been so abusive. She worried about what would happen to her son in his house.

"I'm so frustrated," Fruge had told her lawyer as she sat in jail awaiting sentencing. "I repeatedly get involved with these people who I think are going to be good, productive relationships for me, and they turn out to be exactly the opposite."

Of course, she didn't get the chance to explain anything to the judge. Even if she had, no one would have believed a word. Instead, Barranco continued, telling the judge how shocked he'd been to hear about Fruge's behavior and arrest. "Right now my son only talk about guns and weapons and my son is so afraid of the police and helicopters that my son, when he see the police, he runs."

Fruge denied Barranco's characterizations that she was a negligent parent. Josh had once won an award from the fire department, and Barranco tried to use even that against Fruge. Somehow the candles on an Easter decoration had started a fire in Fruge's kitchen, and Joshua was the first to see it. He ran to the other room to tell his mother, who went to the kitchen and put out the fire.

Barranco also said Fruge had left Joshua at home alone, which wasn't true. She had left him with Raychel once or twice, and the teen-aged Raychel was responsible enough to take care of her little brother for short periods of time.

Before leaving for Fargo, Fruge had obtained a domestic abuse injunction against Barranco, which barred him from contacting her except to arrange visitation. She had pressed charges against him for battery several times. Even as Fruge was sentenced, charges against Barranco were pending in a neighboring county because Barranco had violated the injunction by calling both Gaede and Fruge's mother.

"There is also concern on my client's part that her son be safe and that she be safe, and that has not always been the case, at least with regard to her, in the past based on their relationship and based on prior domestic abuse," Johnson told Hansher at the sentencing hearing. "I think that the thing she is probably most guilty of here ... is making mistake after mistake in choosing with whom she associates in terms of male companions," Johnson said.

Fruge spoke briefly at the sentencing, but her comments belied those she would make later, as she tried to explain her actions immediately following Wicks' murder.

"Yes sir. I would like to say—"

The judge cut her off. "Speak louder. Could you move the microphone closer? I can't hear. Thank you."

Fruge's voice was more audible when she spoke again. "I would like to take this opportunity to apologize for my actions with my son Joshua earlier this year. I sincerely and honestly believe that my son and I were not in any danger at the time, although I certainly understand that I worried my family and they had concerns about us. Furthermore, I have concerns about my son being in the care of his father. I regret that my actions have further complicated my family court situation, and I apologize for any problems that my actions have caused for my son, Joshua. I intend to fully comply with all family court orders and regarding placement and custody of my son in the future. Thank you."

The judge wasn't satisfied. "Did you consider if you were absconding ... and were running with your husband, did you consider leaving him with his father? Didn't you think it was safer to leave him here rather than take him on the road where the authorities were chasing you? Did you consider that or not?"

Fruge nodded. "Yes, I did sir, but at the time my husband was not willing to come back to Milwaukee."

"But you left Milwaukee, though. Didn't you abscond?" the judge asked.

"We were always out of Milwaukee at the time this occurred," she explained. "We were living in North Dakota."

The judge's comments moments later reflect that he either didn't understand what she'd said, or he didn't find it relevant. He specifically cited Fruge's absconding with her son as an aggravating factor of her behavior.

"I understand … her husband didn't want to come back to Milwaukee, but when she made the decision to go on the run or abscond or whatever you want to call it and take her son, she endangered him, and that's a factor the court has to consider," Hansher said.

The judge sentenced Fruge to ten years' probation. She would have to serve the first six months in the House of Correction, starting immediately. She wouldn't be free for Raychel's graduation.

Johnson made a last-ditch effort, asking Hansher to let Fruge serve the six months on house arrest instead of at the House of Correction. The judge said no, adding, "I'm giving her a big enough break the way it is."

Barranco got full custody of Joshua. Fruge would be able to seek supervised visitation with her son upon her release from jail.

The requirement for jail time surprised everyone. Fruge thought of Raychel in her cap and gown and started to cry. Schoonover, who had been waiting in the gallery during the sentencing, felt like crying, too. Although it was within judges' authority to disregard sentencing agreements between the defense and the prosecution, they almost never did.

Schoonover was counting on the fact that Fruge would get straight probation, as the prosecutor had recommended. He'd told the investigators from North Dakota, Cass County Sheriff's Detective Rick Majerus and FBI Special Agent John Dalziel, as much, and they had driven about 575 miles to Milwaukee for the sentencing. They planned to follow Fruge out of the building and convince her to talk. Her return to the House of Correction made that impossible. Instead, Majerus and Dalziel drove back to North Dakota, with Majerus lamenting yet another wasted trip.

Majerus and Dalziel came back to Wisconsin one more time before Fruge was released from jail. But at the last minute, Burdick told them not to talk to her. He didn't want it to appear that her statement had been coerced or made without a lawyer if she was entitled to one, the state's attorney reasoned. So the investigators returned to North Dakota again.

In the summer of 2003, after Fruge was out of jail trying to rebuild her life, the North Dakota authorities drove to Wisconsin a third time. With Schoonover, they arranged to meet with Fruge after her shift working at McDonald's. She got scared and didn't show up.

In November 2003, his patience wearing thin, Schoonover decided to take a run at the suspect for himself. He traveled to the North Dakota State Penitentiary in Bismarck to interview Gaede. Schoonover had hoped to discuss the Milwaukee forgery case and to glean what information he could about the murder. Gaede asked for a lawyer immediately and refused to discuss the forgery. He let Schoonover know, in no uncertain terms, that he blamed the detective for turning Fruge against him. At first, Gaede was so ticked off that he wouldn't sit down. He paced the interrogation room like a caged animal.

Schoonover tried redirecting the conversation. "Tell me about Monroe County," the detective prompted. It was like a light had been switched on. Gaede loosened up and chatted with Schoonover for three hours, telling the detective about some of his past problems in Wisconsin. Gaede wove a tale about dirty cops, corrupt prosecutors and dangerous motorcycle gangsters. Schoonover knew some of the cops Gaede was talking about, so he wasn't buying a word of it, but he let the con man talk.

"Now, how about we talk about these forgeries?" Schoonover tried again.

"No. I need a lawyer for that," Gaede reiterated.

It was really sad, Schoonover thought, that Gaede had chosen to channel his creativity and his superb acting skills toward a life of crime. Gaede could have been quite effective as an undercover police agent and could have built a successful career in law enforcement. Instead, he was on the other side.

In 26 years of police work, Schoonover had never come across a con man quite as smooth as Dennis Gaede. The detective left the Bismarck prison with just one bit of useful information. Gaede did not want to come back to Wisconsin. Maybe some unsavory criminals really were out to get him. Maybe he was just paranoid. Schoonover wasn't sure. The only thing genuine about Gaede that day was his fear of returning to the Badger State.

After that meeting, Schoonover knew Gaede would never crack. He was far too smooth, a big talker who had told the same intricate lies so many times he'd grown to believe them. Fruge was the detective's only hope.

CHAPTER FIFTEEN

Schoonover made it his mission to gain Diana Fruge's trust.

He visited her several times while she was in jail, and those visits continued once she was released. He listened sympathetically as she shared frustrations about her supervised visits with Joshua and her fears about how her son would turn out if he were raised solely by Barranco.

During those conversations, Schoonover took every opportunity to tell Fruge what a loser her husband was. At first, his words had no effect.

Fruge wrote to Gaede about one of the conversations from jail: *Kent Schoonover — the detective from Hales Corners ... was here talking to me yesterday. I told him I couldn't talk until I had a lawyer — he said OK but proceeded to tell me what a bad boy you are. ... He was surprised that I knew everything about you — he asked me if I knew about your kids, your careers in the past, etc. He told me that you never finished any of your degrees, that you are gay, and that you use and manipulate people to get what you want. He said you are doing that with me. He said that I shouldn't be surprised if you break all ties with me because you've already used me up! I'm pretty sure that's not true. If it is, I'm going to feel like a real fool."*

The letter later continued: *Oh, I forgot to tell you — that cop also said that you abused me. When I told him that you never did, he said, 'Give it time.'*

Schoonover's words turned out to be prophetic. As the couple sat in jail, Gaede's hold on Fruge loosened. Her mother, Colleen Anderson, was well aware of Fruge's penchant for choosing abusive and manipulative men, and she encouraged her daughter to walk away from Gaede. Anderson and Fruge never discussed Wicks' death specifically, but Anderson knew Fruge wasn't capable of murder. That left only one alternative suspect in her mind: Gaede.

Gaede's less-than-devoted letters continued to weigh on Fruge as well. He was constantly suspicious that she was flirting with guards or plotting ways to cheat on him.

In my letters I reveal a lot of deep emotion, but yours really don't, he wrote. *That's why I feel like you're holding something back from me. I can't help but feel threatened right now because I'm not there to hold you and help you through this. If I'm wrong tell me or if I'm right tell me.*

He went on to accuse her of getting a guard's phone number and of having too much money in her commissary account: *Are you talking to this guy? Who sent you the money? ... I am really upset about this Diane. ... All I have to say is that after you get this letter the opening paragraph of the next letter you send me better have fucking answers to those questions and I mean all of them or don't bother sending it. Oh, and please tell me that you don't think that guard is hot too. If you do I think that I'll puke.*

Although he always said he was sorry in his next missive, the written apologies were easier to resist than those given in person. Eventually, Fruge filed for divorce.

Her romantic exploits took a different turn while she was in custody in Milwaukee. Fruge had never been attracted to women in the past, but the longer she stayed locked up, the more she thought she'd had enough of men. Trina Thomas was a lesbian and a drug addict who had been in and out of prison for 11 years, yet she was easy for Fruge to love. She was also easy for Fruge to confide in. During one of their many intimate conversations in jail, Fruge told Thomas her secret — the truth.

Fruge and Thomas moved in together when they were released. Fruge was sick of cutting hair, so she got a job at McDonald's. Her paltry salary was barely enough to make the rent. In a relatively short time, Thomas spent the rent money on drugs, Fruge said. They were evicted. For a week, the two women lived together in Fruge's car. Then Thomas met up with an old friend, Manuel, a construction worker who agreed to rent them a room in his rundown duplex on the city's south side.

When Thomas was arrested on a new drug charge, Fruge stayed at Manuel's, making a seamless transition from boarder to girlfriend. Women were easier, relationship-wise, but sex just wasn't the same. Fruge told Thomas as much and promised to always love her as a friend, but Thomas had a hard time accepting it.

Once Thomas was gone, Schoonover got into the habit of stopping by the duplex sometimes, after his shift. He knew it was a gamble. Anyone could construe the meetings as inappropriate — a seasoned detective alone at night with a female suspect. Fruge could make all kinds of accusations against him and it would be his word against hers. But Schoonover couldn't stop making the visits.

One night in January 2004, as he sat on the end of the couch petting one of Manuel's many cats, Schoonover heard the words he'd been hoping for. Fruge told him she was ready to talk. "I finally trust you," she told him. Then the whole story poured out.

Fruge said she never thought Gaede would really kill Wicks. North Dakota wasn't next door to Wisconsin, and it was pretty isolated. He could live there as Wicks, Gaede figured, and his so-called friend would never figure it out. Things started falling apart, however, when Gaede called Wicks in late December 2001, just to chat.

As soon as Gaede hung up the phone, Fruge could tell something was wrong. During the course of the conversation, Wicks had told Gaede someone was using his credit cards. Fruge said Gaede panicked, knowing it was only a matter of time before Wicks discovered the truth.

On December 19, 2001, Fruge's daughter, Raychel, took a train to Fargo to visit her mother and to celebrate her birthday, which was December 22. A few days later, Fruge, Gaede, Raychel and Joshua drove back to Wisconsin and spent Christmas with Fruge's mother and step-father. That night, Fruge and Gaede stayed at the EconoLodge.

135

The next day, Gaede went to pick up Wicks. The plan was already in motion. Gaede had persuaded Wicks to accompany him to Canada, saying he could make $800 a week playing drums. Wicks handed over a copy of his birth certificate, ostensibly so Gaede could process the paperwork to make him eligible for employment in Canada. From his tax business, Gaede already had a copy of Wicks' Social Security card and other personal information.

They traveled in separate cars, Wicks behind Gaede's Buick in his brand-new Cavalier. Wicks didn't have a cell phone, so he used Fruge's to keep in touch on the road to North Dakota.

For the next two nights, Wicks slept on the couch of the Gardner farmhouse. When Gaede went to work at Compressed Air, Wicks helped Fruge unpack and organize the house. Gaede asked Wicks to paint the stairwell, which he did without complaint. Most of his drums stayed in the car, but at one point Wicks brought in a small drum, and he let Joshua bang away. Later, Wicks took a spin to downtown Fargo to pick out some post cards for his family.

Fruge didn't think Gaede could be serious about killing Wicks, a seemingly harmless painter. Gaede would probably bring his friend up north, introduce him to some people in Canada and leave him there, she thought.

By that time, Fruge's brief stay in rehab had ended, and she had switched to non-alcoholic beer. As she contemplated the worst-case scenario that could lie ahead, she went back to regular beer, then to Mike's Hard Lemonade.

The evening of Wicks' murder started out unremarkably. The Christmas tree lights twinkled; Fruge made a big chicken dinner. She had a few beers with Gaede and Wicks, but when the men went down to the basement to smoke some pot, she ushered Joshua upstairs for a bath and bed. She didn't smoke that stuff, and she didn't want her child exposed to it. Mother and son fell asleep. The next thing she knew, Gaede was shaking her. It was close to midnight.

"Come downstairs. Come downstairs."

Half asleep, she followed her husband to the kitchen.

Wicks was lying on the floor between the kitchen and the foyer. He was snoring quietly.

"What did you do?" she asked. "Party him out?"

"No. I shot him."

Fruge was confused. Wicks was breathing. She didn't see any blood.

"He's still alive," she said, sitting down on the couch. She put her head between her knees to keep from passing out. When she looked up, she still didn't believe it.

"If you shot him, why is he still breathing?" she asked.

"I don't know," her husband answered. "I've never seen anything like it in my life."

According to Fruge, Gaede got a plastic bag and walked toward the unconscious man on the floor. She took one last look and finally saw the blood, a fairly small pool seeping from under his head. Then she went to the bathroom and threw up.

Meanwhile, Gaede was frantic. Pacing. Panting. More nervous than she had ever seen him.

"Quit freaking out on me," she admonished him. "I've got a dead man on my kitchen floor."

Her first instinct was to call the police right away, but how could she explain that she was married to one Tim Wicks, but another Tim Wicks was dead on the kitchen floor? What if they thought she had been involved? What would happen to Joshua? What if Gaede didn't want to leave any witnesses?

Gaede wrapped the body in a paint tarp. She helped him drag it about a hundred feet though the snow out to the barn, which had been converted to a three-car garage. Then they went back to the house.

Both put on latex gloves, the kind she had worn while coloring clients' hair. Gaede sopped up the blood splattered on the linoleum where Wicks' head had been. Fruge mopped and scrubbed with Clorox Clean-Up. When they had finished, they threw the gloves, paper towels and dirty rags into a box. Gaede carried the box and Wicks' possessions out to the garage. Then Gaede threw the comforter from the couch where Wicks had slept into the washing machine. Joshua stayed asleep.

From that point on, Fruge stayed drunk — on beer, bourbon, whiskey, whatever she could get her hands on. She stayed in bed, but awake, for more than 24 hours, trying to distract herself and her son with movies and the television.

A few days later, Gaede rented a backhoe to bury the body in the back yard. He stayed outside digging for a couple of hours, but the ground was frozen solid, Fruge said. They visited the Fleet Farm for supplies. Then he rented a U-Haul truck, which they drove to Gaede's cabin in Powers, Michigan.

Fruge said she and Joshua sat in the front seat of the U-Haul truck, parked outside the Michigan cabin, as Gaede dismembered the body in the back. Although the radio was blasting, she could still hear banging and hacking. As Fruge sat with her son, she could imagine Gaede struggling to get the clothes off the frozen body, then doing his best to be sure it was never identified.

Gaede's initial thought was to drop the body down a well on the property, but it was frozen. So they drove to the Menominee River. There, it was pitch dark and eerily quiet. No one was around.

"Get out and help me," Gaede told Fruge.

"Stay right here," she told Joshua. "Mommy's got to help Daddy with something in the back."

It seemed an eternity before Gaede got the body out of the truck. Once he did, she helped him heave it over a guardrail. Joshua tried to snuggle close to her when she got back into the cab, but she refused to hold him until after they had stopped at a gas station to wash up. She stood in

138

front of the mirror in the dingy rest room, staring at her blood-covered clothes in disbelief. She yanked off her black leather jacket. What was she going to do? How could she stay with a killer? How could she leave with no money, no car and a 3-year-old?

After heaving the torso over the guardrail, they drove some more. Along the way, they dumped the boxes and trash bags of bloody tools and rags in different locations. In Milwaukee, they stopped at Gaede mother's Laundromat and gave her some of Wicks' things to get rid of.

According to Fruge, Gaede told his mother, "I had to kill him."

"What's in the bucket?" Hazel asked.

"The head," Gaede replied, "and the hands."

As they headed back to Gardner, they dumped the rest of Wicks' possessions along the way, except his beloved drums. They kept the bucket, too.

Back in home in North Dakota, they unloaded the drums at their farmhouse, then returned the U-Haul. A note left at the house by the sheriff's department set Gaede's nerves on edge. An unfamiliar car was parked across the street, near the grain elevators. Gaede became paranoid, convinced that his former bosses at Compressed Air had hired private detectives to keep an eye on him. He took off in Wicks' car, bringing the head and hands with him. Fruge and her son stayed at the house. When Gaede returned a couple of days later, he told Fruge that he had driven to the Michigan border and thrown Wicks' head in the river and his hands in the woods somewhere, so animals would eat them. She didn't ask for details.

They hit the road again, this time driving Wicks' beloved Cavalier to Milwaukee. Fruge dropped the black Z-24 at the dealership where he had bought it, saying she was Wicks' girlfriend and he could no longer afford the payments. Before anyone could ask questions, she took off.

The couple was at a motel on 27th Street in Milwaukee when the Hales Corners police called Gaede's cell phone number, looking for Wicks. Gaede hurriedly said he was Dennis Johnson from Bismarck, and he didn't know Wicks.

Gaede cleaned out Wicks' bank accounts. They used Wicks' $17,000 inheritance and Fruge's driver's license to buy their RV, she said.

Then Gaede put his wife on a train back to the Gardner farmhouse to collect some of their possessions. At the house, she loaded up Hazel's Buick with her kids' photo albums, plates, towels, blankets, her husband's real and fake IDs, some of Joshua's clothes and two rifles Gaede kept in a closet near the Christmas tree. Gaede wanted to keep Wicks' drums, so she put those back in the car, too. She was on the road back to Milwaukee before the post office across the street opened at 6 a.m., and she reunited with her husband and son later that day. They loaded everything into the RV and dropped off the car with Gaede's mother.

Then they went on the run. They drove for so long she forgot what day it was, what year it was. Every time they came close to a weigh station, Gaede left the freeway, not wanting anyone to remember them. While they were on the road, Gaede came up with a plan: Fruge could tell the police Wicks tried to rape her, so she killed him.

"You won't be convicted," she recalled him saying. "But even if you are, you'll only get eight years because it's self-defense. Then when you get out, we can be together."

The alternative, he told her, would be far worse. If he were to be charged with the crime, there would be no way out. No one would believe his self-defense claim. Wicks was substantially thinner than Gaede and had only been in one minor fight, with his brother-in-law. That would never work. No, if Gaede were charged with the murder of Wicks, he would go away forever, and their marriage would be over.

Fruge couldn't stand the thought of that. Aside from his criminal past, Gaede was the sweetest guy she'd ever been with. He treated her like a queen, and he loved her kids. Even as they were fleeing the law, facing almost inevitable prison time, she believed that maybe they could have a future together. One day, she did as he asked and wrote a confession addressed to the police.

By the time she relayed the story to Schoonover, Fruge realized how lucky she had been. She had been charged with only a child custody violation. She could easily have been charged with murder, manslaughter, or something equally serious. She couldn't believe how gullible she had been.

In his gut, Schoonover knew Fruge was telling the truth this time. Her words were sincere, and her demeanor was as it should be. At times during the story, she cried. At other times, she seemed to have reservations about the next thing she planned to say.

Schoonover returned to the Hales Corners police station, notebook in hand, around 10 p.m. He was elated. He used his notes of Fruge's confession to write a report and immediately sent it to Rick Majerus in Fargo.

CHAPTER SIXTEEN

Fruge said she waited more than two years to tell the police the truth because she feared both Gaede and criminal prosecution. Fruge had hoped DNA or some other physical evidence would conclusively tie Gaede to the murder, and he could be charged without her testimony. As time passed, it became clear to her that wasn't going to happen.

Fruge's conscience also started to bother her. What would her children think when they were old enough to understand their mom let a murderer go free? Worse yet, what if Gaede was never prosecuted and he got out of prison someday? That scenario wasn't outside the realm of possibility. His four-year fraud term in North Dakota would end in August 2005. He still had a sentencing pending in Wisconsin on the old Monroe County charges, but no one knew how much time he would get. Without a murder conviction, he could be walking the streets in a relatively short time.

After Fruge broke down and told Schoonover the truth, she committed herself to putting her ex-husband away. She remained incredibly nervous, however. What if she testified and Gaede got off anyway? What would he do then?

The police were a concern, too. Fruge trusted Schoonover, who said he would do all he could to help her, but the Hales Corners detective didn't carry much weight with Birch Burdick. She didn't have an immunity deal with Burdick or with any of the prosecutors in the numerous jurisdictions where she and her ex-husband had done illegal things. On her McDonald's salary, she didn't have enough money to hire a lawyer. Since she wasn't facing charges, she wasn't eligible for a public defender. She was out on a limb, hoping the authorities would be merciful.

Fruge also had few people to confide in. Although she attended Alcoholics Anonymous meetings, it didn't seem the appropriate place to talk about her life of crime. She had become somewhat estranged from her sisters and mother after the debacle with Barranco. Things with Manuel were still new. Trina Thomas was on her way back to prison. Schoonover became Fruge's main source of support.

After Fruge was convicted of the child custody charge, Joshua was placed with his father. Every few weeks, Fruge went back to family court trying to get more visitation time. She also wanted the court to allow her to see her son without a court official keeping an eye on them. Every time, even with Schoonover speaking on her behalf, the judge refused.

In February 2004, not long after Fruge's revelation to Schoonover, Cass County Sheriff's Deputy Majerus finally got his chance at the elusive witness. Fruge sat down for a formal, videotaped interview with him and the FBI's Dalziel. Schoonover was along for moral support but didn't ask any questions.

The interview lasted three hours, with Fruge taking occasional breaks to smoke a Newport. She was nervous. She had a hard time remembering the types of details the cops were looking for — the dates when certain things occurred and the routes she and Gaede had taken on their drive around the country. At certain points, she asked the men for help. At others, they pointed out that in light of other evidence, she was probably mistaken.

Afterward, she vented her frustrations in a letter to Thomas.

Dear Trina,

Hi, honey. I have had a stressful day. First court this a.m. Brando demolished my reputation in court. He called me the murderer. I was hoping to get unsupervised visitation but ... he was screaming like a maniac that I was going to kidnap his son again. He was such a jackass. He is the anti-Christ I believe. I have another hearing on April 28 th. I hope by then I can prove my credibility.

Next I met with the FBI, Schoonover, and a lieutenant from North Dakota. I told them the whole story, beginning to end. Even what I was guilty of.

I gave them your name, (since) they were asking who I have told. Please be honest with them and tell them the truth. I already have confessed and they want to verify that I am telling the truth. They know about the disposal and everything.

I need to put Dennis Gaede away forever or he'll come and he'll kill me. Please cooperate with them. And, yes, they do know about our relationship.

Later on I will be going to Minneapolis to take a polygraph. Today I was videotaped. Next, I will be going with the FBI to show them places, routes and put a timeline together. I can only pray for the best.

How are you doing? ... I miss you, baby. I am always going to love you, Trina. Please keep in touch with me.

Love, Diane

Fruge's promise to drive around the country with the FBI along the route she, Gaede and Joshua took in the RV wasn't helpful since they had driven in circles a lot and she had been drunk much of the time. She took the lie detector test and passed. She even did extensive interviews with television and print reporters about Gaede's crime and her part in helping to cover it up.

Schoonover felt that once the authorities had Fruge's statement, they had a winnable case. He also realized cases weakened over time. Files got dusty. Witnesses' memories faded. Schoonover did not want that to happen this time. Even if they took the case to a jury and lost, he felt they had to give it a try. They owed it to Wicks. But it wasn't up to him.

By July 2004, two years after Wicks' death and five months after Fruge's confession, Schoonover had lost hope that Gaede would ever be charged with murder. Burdick grew tired of Schoonover's nagging.

There were several barriers to a murder charge, the worst of which remained proving jurisdiction. Before Fruge came forward, no one knew where Wicks was killed. Charges could only be issued in the county where the crime occurred. Guess wrong, and the defendant would walk. That meant that if Gaede was going to be charged with murder, it had to be in Cass County, North Dakota, according to Fruge's account of the crime.

The only evidence authorities had to prove jurisdiction was Fruge's word, and she wasn't the best witness. She had a criminal history, albeit a minor one. She had repeatedly confessed to Wicks' murder herself, a fact that a skilled defense attorney could use to attack her credibility. Her drinking was another problem. It made her memories sketchy. Despite their best efforts, local, state and federal authorities had not found a shred of physical evidence to corroborate her story.

Although Fruge and Gaede had since divorced, the fact that they were once married posed another problem. Although she was willing to testify against him, North Dakota law limited how much she could say. She wouldn't be allowed testify about things he told her, only about what she saw.

The limited prosecutorial experience with murder trials in North Dakota also was problematic. There are only about 10 murders a year in the state, most of them domestic.

Majerus thought he'd brought Burdick a great circumstantial case, but he knew that Burdick and other prosecutors liked hard evidence. Majerus was starting to think they might never find any. There were no leads on the location of Wicks' hands. Majerus doubted they would ever be found without detailed directions to their whereabouts, and maybe not even then. The Gardner farmhouse had been sold and the garage torn down. The detective was continually frustrated by the misconceptions of law enforcement perpetuated by television crime shows, in which a crime, arrest, conviction and jail sentence are all wrapped up in a tidy package. In real life, it was never that easy.

As the months passed, Wicks' family also lost hope that Gaede would ever be brought to justice. Neary, a tool and die maker, worked part time for the mounted police in Wisconsin's state capitol, Madison. Neary and his horse, Quest, would patrol events like the big Halloween party near the University of Wisconsin campus and the state fair outside Milwaukee. Through that job, Neary got to know a lot of homicide detectives, and sometimes he discussed Wicks' case with them. The consensus was clear: Gaede's past work as a police officer just might help him get off. Gaede knew what kind of evidence was needed for a murder conviction, and he apparently knew how to get rid of it.

Burdick always took Neary's telephone calls, but the conversations were less than encouraging. "Without a smoking gun, all we have is circumstantial evidence," Neary recalls him saying. "Juries want DNA, hard evidence, like on CSI," he said, alluding to the popular television show. "Without that, there's no case."

"But we know Gaede did it," Neary protested.

"Knowing it is one thing. Proving it is another," the prosecutor replied.

CHAPTER SEVENTEEN

Time was running out. Gaede was scheduled to be released from prison on the North Dakota embezzlement charges in August 2005. Five months before his release date, Wisconsin authorities had no idea if or when Gaede would be charged in North Dakota for the murder of Timothy Wicks. So they decided to do what they could to keep him behind bars.

In March, Gaede was transported from the North Dakota state prison in Bismarck to Monroe County, Wisconsin. There, he was to be sentenced for his old crimes, the ones that had caused him to flee to North Dakota and live as Wicks in the first place.

Gaede had fled to North Dakota after the trial, he told the court, because he worried about what would happen to Fruge if he went to prison. His only motivation for leaving the state was to get his wife into rehab for her alcohol abuse. Once she was well, he had planned to come back.

Monroe County Circuit Judge Steven Abbott sentenced Gaede to five years in prison, to be served immediately after his North Dakota time. If Gaede earned credit for good behavior, he could finish the sentence in three years.

It was looking more and more like the Milwaukee County forgery charges were the best hope of keeping Gaede locked up for a significant period of time. He faced up to 15 years on each of three charges for signing Wicks' name on withdrawal slips at M&I Bank branches.

Milwaukee prosecutors didn't know it, but time for pursuing those charges was about to expire due to a little-known and complicated Wisconsin law. The law said that if a defendant, imprisoned in another state, informs Wisconsin prosecutors of his whereabouts and requests the resolution of his case, he must be brought to trial within 180 days. On October 8, 2004, Gaede signed a document that did both of those things, but it listed only his Monroe County charges. The warden of the Bismarck prison, Tim Schuetzle, sent that notice only to Monroe County, where the district attorney received it 10 days later. No one told Milwaukee officials until after Gaede's sentencing in March. As Monroe County authorities prepared to transport Gaede back to Bismarck, Monroe County Assistant District Attorney Jennifer Harper noticed the pending Milwaukee charges and called her counterpart there to see if Gaede should be sent to Milwaukee instead of North Dakota. By then, there were only six weeks remaining in the 180-day time period.

The law said prisoners couldn't be shuttled back and forth from state to state. Therefore, if Gaede were sent back to North Dakota, the forgery charges would have to be dropped altogether.

Milwaukee authorities scrambled to get Gaede to Milwaukee for his first court appearance, the formal reading of the forgery charges. Then, inexplicably, he sat in the Milwaukee County Jail for two months.

Gaede had run out of money and could not pay his favorite attorney, Bridget Boyle, this time. Instead, he was assigned Maureen Fitzgerald, a public defender. Unfortunately for the state, Fitzgerald was just as effective as Gaede's former high-priced, high-profile criminal lawyer. In early May, Fitzgerald brought a motion to dismiss the forgery charges, claiming that Gaede's civil rights had been violated because he didn't get a trial within 180 days. A nervous Schoonover sat in the gallery and listened to the proceedings.

Milwaukee County prosecutors argued that because Gaede's October letter mentioned only the Monroe County charges and not those in Milwaukee, the letter hadn't started the clock for them. They believed Harper's phone call five months later should have served as their notice, leaving plenty of time to get to trial.

Fitzgerald disagreed. Under the statute, the inmate doesn't have to notify prosecutors in different counties separately, she said. The inmate only has to notify the state, and Gaede had.

Assistant District Attorney DeAnn Heard tried to introduce evidence of Wicks' murder. "The defendant is a prime suspect in—" she began. Fitzgerald objected before Heard could finish her sentence. Milwaukee County Circuit Judge Jean DiMotto agreed with Fitzgerald, both at that moment and at the end of the hearing. The judge dismissed the three felony forgery charges with prejudice, meaning she barred them from being filed again.

Schoonover felt like his guts had been ripped out. The prosecutors immediately asked for an appeal and asked that Gaede stay in Wisconsin while it was pending. DiMotto agreed to read their briefs quickly and rule in a couple of days, giving the prosecutors and Schoonover a shred of hope.

Was it possible that DiMotto didn't know how potentially devastating her decision was? How could she do this, knowing a killer could soon walk free? Schoonover had to talk to the judge. He had to make her understand. DiMotto paused as Schoonover approached and asked to talk to her.

"I assume it's not about this case?" he recalls her saying.

"Well, actually, it is," he answered.

The judge told the detective such a conversation wouldn't be appropriate and walked away.

Two days later, Assistant District Attorney Gilbert Urfer filed the prosecution's motion, which said Gaede had intentionally filed his letter with only Monroe County in order to avoid the Milwaukee forgery charges.

"Mr. Gaede should not be allowed to manipulate the system this way to avoid legitimate prosecution," Urfer wrote. "The only reason for the supposed delay (of Gaede's forgery trial) is Mr. Gaede's own attempts to hide the ball."

Urfer asked that Gaede remain in Wisconsin until the Court of Appeals decided his case. Otherwise, the appeal would be academic, since the law forbade moving prisoners back and forth from state to state.

On May 12, Judge DiMotto read about her ruling in the *Milwaukee Journal Sentinel.* "Slaying Suspect Could Go Free," the headline read. "Judge Throws Out Forgery Charges on Technicality." It was DiMotto's first indication that Gaede was a murder suspect who might never be charged.

Later that day, the judge called the attorneys into court to tell them her decision. She was much harsher on the district attorney's office than she had been at the first hearing, saying prosecutors should have been more diligent, especially since it was such an important case. If they had asked for a delayed trial date due to the late notification by Monroe County, DiMotto said, she would have granted it, and they could have avoided any problems.

"The district attorney outright blew it by not asking for a continuance," she said. "That mistake can't be visited on Mr. Gaede. ... It's not his screw up, and I can't ... hold it against him."

DiMotto refused to order Gaede to remain in Wisconsin pending appeal. With her ruling, the forgery charges were dropped, and the potential for Gaede to serve another 15 to 45 years in prison disappeared.

Wicks' family was devastated.

"If this guy gets out, I'm going to take him out," Neary told his mother-in-law.

"That would be wonderful, but then you would be jeopardizing your soul," she replied.

Neary considered himself a kind and gentle man. Unlike many Wisconsin natives, who look forward to hunting season every year, Neary wouldn't even consider hurting an innocent animal. Gaede, though, was a different story. "If he showed up, I would kill him," Wicks' brother-in-law vowed.

CHAPTER EIGHTEEN

Time marched on. Gaede's prison term on the theft and fraud charges drew to an end. He would be released from the North Dakota prison in a matter of days. Schoonover knew that once Gaede was sent back to Wisconsin, the odds of murder charges being filed against him in Fargo would decrease dramatically.

Schoonover didn't know that Burdick and his assistant, Mark Boening, had thought long and hard about murder charges. Before Fruge spoke out, they knew they didn't have a case. Afterward, they urged Majerus and the other Cass County investigators to find as much corroborating evidence as possible. For the prosecution, the timing of the charge was crucial. If they went to court too soon and lost, they could never try Gaede again, even if they found a smoking gun.

By August 2005, Burdick and Boening figured the odds of their case getting any better were slim. They knew they could lose the case, but decided to give it their best shot. On August 3, 2005, Burdick charged Gaede with Wicks' murder. A conviction could mean Gaede would spend the rest of his life in prison without the possibility of parole. The harshest penalty in the state, life without parole had been handed down just once or twice in Fargo since the state legislature had approved it about a decade earlier.

Almost four years had passed since Wicks' dismembered body had been identified. At a Fargo news conference, Burdick said the complexity of the crime warranted a long investigation and thorough review before charges could be issued. The case had generated more than 2,000 pages of documentation and required the cooperation of law enforcement officers in three states, as well as the FBI. "There has been a long and intricate investigation by authorities here and in Wisconsin and Michigan. It's extensive. (Today) we believed it was appropriate to go ahead and file the charges," he said.

Schoonover, who had received word that he would be called as a prosecution witness, was ecstatic. Fruge, who had gotten the same word, was terrified. She dreaded the thought of facing her ex-husband in court.

Within days, Gaede was moved from the North Dakota state penitentiary in Bismarck to the Cass County Jail in Fargo. The case was assigned to Judge Steven E. McCullough, who set bail at $500,000. Gaede, who made his first court appearance on the murder charge via videoconference from the jail, asked that Monte Mertz be allowed to represent him. Mertz had served as Gaede's lawyer in the Compressed Air case. McCullough said no. Indigent defendants have the right to an attorney, he said, but not the right to the attorney of their choosing.

Instead of Mertz, McCullough assigned another public defender, Steven D. Mottinger, to the case. Mottinger was known for the black 10-gallon hat and cowboy boots he wore to court. He also walked with a slight limp. Born in 1952, Mottinger grew up in Robbinsville, Minnesota, a suburb of Minneapolis. He earned his bachelor's degree from St. John's University in nearby Collegeville, where he majored in government. Later, in his opening statement in the Gaede case, he would tell jurors about studying the philosophy of Immanuel Kant in an ethics and logic class.

Mottinger didn't want to spend his life teaching and didn't aspire to run for office, the two main careers one could pursue with a government degree. He decided to go to law school because "it was the '70s. It was kind of the thing to do," he said. He chose the William Mitchell College of Law in St. Paul, Minnesota and graduated in 1979.

Mottinger often joked that he relocated to North Dakota after law school for a lot of reasons, better duck hunting among them. In truth, he felt comfortable in Fargo, which wasn't far from the small southwestern Minnesota town where his parents grew up. As a child, he'd spent a lot of time on a family farm there, and he still had many friends in the area. He liked the rural lifestyle with its hunting and fishing, the small-town sensibility, the wide-open spaces.

Mottinger was the first to admit he became a defense lawyer by accident. His first job as an attorney was in Beech, North Dakota, helping another lawyer. Soon he realized he didn't want to spend the next 60 years writing wills and waiting for something to happen. So when he got a call from Montana Legal Services about a job he'd applied for while back in school, he took it. That's where he started wearing the trademark cowboy hat, and he never stopped.

About three years later, in 1983, Ronald Regan was president and the specter of budget cuts was looming large. A friend called Mottinger to let him know that the man who had the public defender contract in Fargo was looking for help. Mottinger applied and was hired. He liked the idea of being the final buffer that stood between his client and an unforgiving government.

The job was never boring. In one of his early cases, Mottinger asked a witness if she could identify a man who had been flashing people in a hospital parking ramp. The confused woman said yes and pointed right at Mottinger.

Mottinger also once represented a group of gypsies charged with robbing some Vietnamese restaurateurs.

"Nobody could speak English," he recalled for a profile in the county newsletter. "It was, to say the least, a mess!" The judge dismissed the case after the preliminary hearing. Mottinger was as relieved as his clients.

As the years went by, Mottinger found himself having less fun on the job. Things at the courthouse became more formal, and the cases got more serious. Mottinger was sad to see ever-increasing numbers of drug and sexual assault cases. The murder cases often haunted him.

One murder defendant Mottinger represented was housed in a secure area of the jail because of a history of assaulting guards. For safety reasons, Mottinger wasn't allowed to meet with his client in the attorney conference room and had to talk to him separated by bars. "The first time I saw him he held out his hand through the bars and said, 'I bet you're afraid of this and won't shake my hand,'" Mottinger recalled. "Of course I had to, did, and never had a bit of trouble from him after that."

By the time Mottinger met Gaede, the defense lawyer was already familiar with the facts of the case, as were most others involved in Cass County's legal system. Early on, Mottinger explained to his client that while the state's case was graphically strong, it was factually weak. By graphically strong he meant it was a sensational crime with a mutilated body, the crossing of state lines, and all kinds of lurid detail that grabbed headlines. Mottinger didn't worry too much about that. In his experience, people paid attention to fresh news, but as time went by, they tended to forget things. They would have forgotten a lot, Mottinger predicted, by the time jury selection came around.

As for the factual weaknesses, there were many. With no physical evidence and a star witness who had confessed to the crime several times, Mottinger figured they had at least a 50/50 shot at winning at trial.

Gaede, who listened attentively as Mottinger explained their options, wasn't like many of the people Mottinger had represented over the past two decades. Gaede was a gentleman. He always spoke politely to Mottinger's secretary and paralegals. When Mottinger was busy with other clients, Gaede didn't lose his temper. He cooperated fully with the defense investigators.

From the beginning, Mottinger was intrigued by the case. On one hand, there usually weren't any eyewitnesses to murder. On the other hand, he had never before tried a homicide case in which there was not one scintilla of physical evidence. In most cases, the location of the crime was obvious. The prosecution just had to prove who did it, why and how. Usually, the defense attorney's job was simply to prove his guy wasn't there. In this case, proving that the murder might not have occurred in Cass County would be enough to get Gaede acquitted.

In criminal cases in North Dakota, defendants had the right to a preliminary hearing. There, prosecutors had to show it was more likely than not that a crime was committed and that the defendant committed it. The standard was called probable cause, and it was far less than the proof required at trial. For that reason, most defendants tended to waive the right to a preliminary hearing, believing it was probably a waste of time.

Not Gaede. He insisted on a preliminary hearing. Assistant State's Attorney Mark Boening, known for prosecuting some of the county's most difficult cases, appeared for the prosecution.

Boening grew up in southern Minnesota and earned his bachelor's degree at Gustavus Adolphus College, a small, liberal-arts school in St. Peter, Minnesota. He earned his law degree in 1982 at the University of North Dakota in Grand Forks and then practiced law in the western North Dakota town of Dickinson. Boening joined the Cass County state's attorney's office three years later in the child support enforcement division. Since 1990, he had worked exclusively on criminal cases and was known for winning some tough ones.

One of the most sensational murder cases Boening had tried took place back in 1999, the year Burdick took office. Kyle Bell, a sex offender who had served prison time for molesting his nieces and nephews, was the prime suspect in the kidnapping and murder of 11-year-old Jeanna North. Jeanna disappeared in June 1993 after roller-blading with a friend, then heading home alone. Bell, who had been living near Jeanna's family in Fargo, confessed to molesting the girl and killing her in his garage. He said he tied a cement block to her body and threw it off a bridge into the Sheyenne River.

Bell later recanted, and a federal court ruled the confession could not be used at trial. Majerus and his colleagues at the Cass County Sheriff's Department searched the river 15 times. They even dammed the river once to stop its flow in hopes that it would be easier to find Jeanna's body without the current. It didn't work. The body was never found.

Boening and two other prosecutors tried the murder case anyway, using parts of the confession that Bell had repeated to police voluntarily as the primary evidence against him. Bell, represented by Mottinger, was convicted and sentenced to life in prison.

Going into the Bell case, Boening wasn't sure he would win a conviction. He felt the same way about the Gaede case.

At Gaede's preliminary hearing, Boening presented Judge Steven E. McCullough with a copy of the criminal complaint, which detailed the version of events Fruge had shared with Schoonover.

Mottinger called both Majerus and the FBI's Dalziel to testify. Through questioning, the defense attorney emphasized that there was no physical evidence linking Gaede to the crime — not in the Gardner house, not in the garage, not in the U-Haul truck. Mottinger also tried to have the case thrown out on jurisdiction. Wicks' body was found in Wisconsin and Michigan. The only indication that he was murdered in North Dakota was from Fruge, who had repeatedly confessed to committing the crime herself. Her statements were corroborated, Majerus testified, only by circumstantial evidence and by the statements of a few jailhouse snitches.

Mottinger drove his points home as he tried to convince McCullough to dismiss the murder charge. "We're not arguing that a crime was committed someplace. The decedent's body was found in several pieces in another jurisdiction. Obviously he didn't do that to himself. ... But the bottom line is there's no evidence to support her statement that's been offered that would give the court any inference that a crime has been committed here in Cass County. There's just not enough here," Mottinger argued.

McCullough disagreed and refused to dismiss the case. Gaede pleaded not guilty, and his bail was continued at half a million dollars.

Boening reported back to his boss. The two prosecutors agreed that without physical evidence, it would be hard to get a jury to convict Gaede. They also knew it was unlikely that Gaede would ever plead guilty to murder. They weren't willing to bargain down to anything less. Armed with the glimpse of the defense strategy Mottinger had revealed during the preliminary hearing, they started gearing up to face him at trial.

"He's a great defense lawyer," Burdick cautioned Neary and the rest of Wicks' family. "It's going to be a tough case."

CHAPTER NINETEEN

The 1996 film "Fargo" put the North Dakota town on the map for many Americans — even though most of the movie takes place in Minnesota. In it, a man hires two bumbling hit men to kidnap his wife. Things go wrong, leading to murder. The Cohen brothers' classic features a pregnant police detective, Marge Gunderson, memorably portrayed by Frances McDormand, who won an Academy Award for the role. The actors' regional accents, amusing in their authenticity to outsiders, seem a bit overdone to the locals, as does a bloody scene featuring a wood chipper.

The town's residents have an uneasy respect for the film that made Fargo famous. On one hand, the investigators and witnesses in the Gaede case envisioned themselves as characters in a sequel, catapulted to notoriety by the bizarre case. On the other hand, Schoonover once made a joke about a wood chipper to Tammy Lynk. She was not amused.

For Gaede's trial, Wisconsinites descended on Fargo. Cass County picked up the tab for Fruge and her daughter, Raychel, to fly back to the scene of the crime since they would both be called as witnesses. Schoonover drove his unmarked detective car from Milwaukee, since he didn't know how long the trial would last. All three, as well as the other out-of-town witnesses in the case, stayed at the Howard Johnson's on the edge of Fargo. Trains rumbled by the motel at all hours of the night, and workers noisily emptied the Dumpsters early in the morning. Nobody got much sleep. Things got really interesting when witnesses on opposite sides of the case ran into each other at the indoor swimming pool. Apparently the fancier Radisson Hotel, across from the Fargo Police station, had rates too high for the county's budget.

Fruge had to take unpaid leave from her minimum-wage job at McDonald's to make the trip. The extremely difficult task of testifying, however, was brightened by the fact that Raychel would be there. When Fruge's legal problems started, her ex-husband had moved to Louisiana, taking their daughter with him. Fruge had not seen her daughter in almost two years. Raychel, 18 years old by the time of the trial, was still overweight, but she seemed confident. Her long dark hair fell straight down her back. In spite of North Dakota's chilly April days, she wore short skirts, t-shirts and flip-flops.

As Raychel arrived in Fargo, she was poised to graduate from high school. She worked part-time in a restaurant attached to a golf course. Her grades were stellar, and she planned to go to law school after college.

Fruge was overjoyed to see her daughter again. The two shared a room at the Howard Johnson's. They made a point of having dinner at Red Lobster on the county's tab. One evening after testimony had ended for the day, mother and daughter visited the mall where they'd done their Christmas shopping shortly before Wicks' death. Fruge cruised by the Zales jewelry store, but didn't see the manager who had reportedly propositioned Gaede.

Tom and Beth Neary arrived in Fargo on Monday, the day jury selection began. Before Wicks' death, they had never considered visiting North Dakota. Beth was surprised at how much Fargo reminded her of northern Wisconsin. Settled mostly by Swedes, Norwegians, Icelanders and Germans, Fargo had a homey, Midwestern feel. Still, the Nearys didn't plan to hang around — not even for the whole trial. The only thing they were interested in was Fruge's testimony. They wanted to know exactly what had happened to Wicks, and they wanted to be sure Fruge did her part to put Gaede away.

Wicks' elderly parents weren't in any condition to make the trip. After Wicks was murdered, his father had suffered serious depression, then a series of mini-strokes. His health had continued to deteriorate. Caring for him had taken a toll on his wife.

162

In nearly every homicide case, someone who knew the victim well is called to testify in order to humanize the victim for the jury. During Gaede's trial, the task would fall to Beth Neary's husband, Tom, since Beth was shy and soft-spoken.

As the trial began, Boening was still stinging from the jury verdict in the case of Kenneth Jacob Jr. a few months before. Jacob, a trucker from Minnesota, had stopped briefly at a Fargo tavern to see his brother. When he left the bar, he backed his empty asphalt truck over Stephen Nelson, 52, who was drunk and passed out in the parking lot. Nelson died. Jacob drove away. Boening had charged murder. Mottinger had argued that Nelson's death was an accident. The jury sided with Mottinger and found Jacob guilty only of leaving the scene of a fatal accident. He would serve only five years in prison.

Boening hoped he and Burdick would fare better with the Gaede case, but a conviction wasn't a sure thing. The prosecutors' biggest fear was Gaede's charm. The defendant was so personable that if he testified, surely the jurors would grow to like him. If they liked him, the differences between his story and Fruge's could be enough to provide reasonable doubt. It was a toss-up, the prosecution knew. A jury could go either way.

On the first day of jury selection, Fargo was in the throes of a flood of epic proportions. The Red River, which forms the border between North Dakota and Minnesota, was inundated with rain and melting snow. The waters crested at 37 feet — which was 19 feet above flood stage and just two feet shy of the 1997 flood, the worst the city had seen in a century.

The Army Corps of Engineers was busy building emergency levees. The sheriff's department sent deputies in boats to check on families in rural areas. Volunteers filled 40-pound sandbags and constructed makeshift dikes around the city. A bridge not far from the Cass County Courthouse was closed, overwhelmed by the floodwaters.

Judge McCullough worried that potential jurors might stay away because of the weather. His fears turned out to be unfounded. Potential jurors showed up in full force, as did droves of reporters. In addition to the beat reporter who regularly covered Cass County's courts for the local paper, the *Fargo Forum*, and the Associated Press' North Dakota correspondent, a newspaper reporter from Milwaukee and a radio reporter from Winnipeg were in attendance. All of the local television stations, too, were hoping to set up cameras in the tiny courtroom.

McCullough banished the television cameras to an empty courtroom downstairs, complete with a video feed of the proceedings. That eased the crowding some, but the courtroom remained fairly cramped quarters.

Mottinger wore a burgundy sport coat, charcoal grey pants and his trademark black cowboy hat. "It's a case we should win, but might not," Mottinger told reporters before jury selection began.

"What are you looking for in a jury?" the *Forum* reporter asked the defense attorney.

"I just want 12 people who are fair and impartial and believe everything I say," Mottinger joked.

Potential jurors walked through a metal detector at the front door of the courthouse. A sheriff's deputy hand checked their bags. When they entered the courtroom, one was dismissed immediately because he wasn't an American citizen. Another was reprimanded for chewing gum.

Mottinger questioned the potential jurors from the defense table, keeping his attitude folksy and casual.

"What did you think when you got your jury notice?" he asked a man who said he worked as an information technologies director.

"Oh, great," the man answered honestly.

"Everybody agree with that?" Mottinger asked the rest.

They nodded and smiled. A few even chuckled.

"What do you like to do for hobbies?" Mottinger continued.

The man hesitated, and then answered: "Drink beer." This time, Mottinger nodded. "An admirable hobby," he said. Mottinger continued, questioning members of the group about the presumption of innocence and reasonable doubt as he tried to figure out which ones might let his client go free.

McCullough dismissed several people. Some knew one of the witnesses, some said they couldn't be objective, some had criminal records, and some said sitting in court for over a week would be too much of a hardship on their jobs or families. Mottinger and Burdick also were allowed to dismiss 10 people each from the jury pool without giving a reason. Before the lunch break rolled around, there were no potential jurors left in the gallery.

"This has never happened before," McCullough said when he realized there was no one left for the lawyers to question. He called his bosses in Bismarck for guidance. They told him to have the clerk call in more potential jurors, those who had been scheduled to show up for a different trial the following day.

Once Mottinger had finished questioning the newcomers, Burdick got his turn. Jury selection was one of Burdick's strongest skills. He had even taught classes about it at the National Advocacy Center, a training facility for prosecutors located at the University of South Carolina.

He took his place behind the podium. "How many people made it through the third grade?" he asked. "Raise your hands." The jurors' hands went up.

"Good," Burdick declared. "Everybody has an arm that works. If I ask a question, raise your hand if you have an answer. There are no right answers to these questions. The answers are whatever you're thinking and you're feeling."

The state's attorney continued, using questions to explain the difference between direct and circumstantial evidence; between actual innocence and the presumption of innocence.

A woman who said her hobbies were watching TV, reading, playing the piano, and sewing had a little trouble understanding some of the terminology. "I'm feeling kind of stupid right now," she said to Burdick at one point.

Still, he pressed on: "Is there a difference between 'without a doubt' or 'without a reasonable doubt'?"

The woman looked at him quizzically. "I have to take out 'reasonable,' just in my own head, to understand the concept," she finally told him.

By the time 12 jurors and two alternates had been selected, it was after 5 p.m. The windowless courtroom was stifling, and the reporters were bored. Eight women and six men would decide Gaede's fate. The men included the information technologies director whose favorite hobby was drinking beer, an agriculture marketing director, an engineering technician who also described himself as a musician, and a carpenter. Among the women was a day care teacher whose father was a minister, a stay-at-home mother of four who was also a dance team coach, and the advertising account executive who said she wasn't sure of the difference between "without a doubt" and "without a reasonable doubt." Another woman juror was divorced, and Mottinger had served as her ex-husband's lawyer during the proceedings. The woman who would become foreperson was an emergency room nurse.

Gaede, in an orange-and-white striped polo shirt and khakis, serenely scrutinized the group as McCullough reminded them not to read the newspaper, watch the news on television, or listen to anything about the case on the radio. "I appreciate your willingness to come in and sit in a hot, sweaty courtroom for a day," he said in closing. "Without your sacrifice, our system does not work."

CHAPTER TWENTY

Was Diana Fruge a weak-willed woman who stood by her man out of love, or was she a killer? That's the question jurors would ponder as they listened to three days of testimony.

Tom Neary was convinced that Gaede was the real killer, but he struggled with his feelings about Fruge. He believed that deep down, she was a good person. Yet he blamed her for being weak and drunk, an emotional wreck who neither warned Wicks about Gaede's plans nor tried to save him.

As opening arguments began in McCullough's tiny courtroom, Neary, Fruge, Raychel, and the other witnesses sat in the law library under a sequestration order that prohibited them from sitting in the courtroom until after they had finished testifying. The idea was to keep them from being influenced by other people's testimony.

Fruge and Raychel sat laughing, talking and catching up on all they'd missed in the two years since they last saw each other.

Neary stewed. He couldn't believe Fruge was sitting there laughing, like everything was fine. "I need to yell at you right now," he said, getting to his feet. "You could have prevented this, and you didn't. You're just as guilty as he is! You're acting like it's all fine now and it's not. Who the hell are you to laugh and act like everything's all right?"

Fruge burst into tears. Neary would have yelled some more, but Schoonover stepped in. "You know, without her, we couldn't even have this trial. She's doing the right thing now."

Fruge looked at the dead man's brother-in-law. "I'm sorry," she told him.

"That's not going to cut it," Neary muttered. But his anger had dissipated even before Schoonover made a final, chilling comment: "If he gets off, he will kill her. And he'll get away with it."

In the courtroom, Burdick, Boening and Mottinger were oblivious to the mini-drama in the law library. For them, it was show time in the courtroom.

Boening spoke first: "As you know, this is a murder case. It is a case which is based on the testimony of the woman who loved the defendant at the time the defendant committed the murder, and this case is based on compelling, corroborating circumstantial evidence."

From there, the assistant prosecutor laid out a chronology of the case, beginning with the discovery of Wicks' body. Like any good lawyer, Boening highlighted the major problems with his own case so jurors would hear about them from him instead of Mottinger.

Fruge made a statement to authorities, Boening said, a statement that she repeated to a fellow inmate in jail in Nebraska, during which she confessed to killing Wicks. "She said that she had killed Tim Wicks. She said that Wicks had come to her residence. Wicks had raped her. He had forced sex upon her. After raping her, she took out a shotgun. ... She shot Wicks in the stomach with the shotgun. ... And then after shooting him, she cut off Tim Wicks' hands and head and tried to stuff Tim Wicks' body into a washing machine in Gardner, North Dakota.

"Well, after hearing that, no doubt all of you are kind of wondering what you're doing here because we have a confession from Diane ... to the crime that we have the defendant charged with. And so why are we sitting here?"

Boening then answered his own question. Fruge's confession didn't hold water, he said, because Wicks was shot with a pistol, not a shotgun. He was shot in the head, not the stomach. And finally, according to the autopsy report, Wicks' head and hands were not removed right away. They had remained intact until after Wicks' body was frozen.

168

Later in his opening, Boening pointed out the other major problem with the state's case: the lack of physical evidence. The circumstantial evidence, however, would corroborate Fruge's testimony, he said. "After you hear and consider all the evidence in this case, the state submits there is but one inescapable conclusion, and that is that this defendant, this man, Dennis Gaede, killed Tim Wicks." Boening waved a hand toward Gaede, who remained impassive. The expression on his face betrayed nothing.

Mottinger, wearing a pink and blue striped tie that didn't quite match his cowboy boots, stood, as humble and folksy as he had been the day before. "That was quite an opening statement," he began. "I am a sometimes student of history, and one of the people I admire is Harry Truman. Harry Truman, as you know, was president of the United States immediately after Franklin Roosevelt. He left office in 1952. He was in his late 60s at that point so he obviously grew up at an earlier time, and he sometimes used not necessarily stories but reminiscences about his earlier life to make a point. And he once said something to the effect that whenever you hear somebody praying too loud in your front yard, you better run out back and make sure the smokehouse is locked.

"I think that that little story is appropriate to a case like this," Mottinger continued. "At this time and at this moment, you are standing in judgment over a fellow human being. Despite the fact that the prosecutors would turn him into some kind of a monster, we believe that he's not.

"It's my privilege this morning to stand here and speak to you on behalf of Dennis Gaede, my client. It is, as I perceive it, the most awesome responsibility that any lawyer could have. I am not going to shrink away from that responsibility. But you know what? I wish I was a better lawyer. I wish I wasn't quite so afraid. I wish I wasn't so afraid I won't be able to live up to the trust and the faith that Dennis Gaede has placed in me. All I can do for him and, yes, for you and, yes, for them, too — all I can do is to do my best, and it has to be good enough because despite what Mr. Boening has outlined to you this morning, they just don't have a case. They cannot prove what they have to prove in order to get a conviction."

Mottinger went on to tell the story of the boy who cried wolf. Fruge, he said, cried wolf too many times to be believed. Without physical evidence to back up her testimony, her story about Gaede killing Wicks wasn't enough to convict Gaede. Mottinger contended that Fruge had killed Wicks herself and confessed to several people. Then she got scared of being sent to prison and changed her story.

"Over 2,000 years ago a man named Judas sold the life of his friend for 30 pieces of silver," Mottinger said. "Just as that betrayal was based on the personal gain of Judas, the betrayal of Dennis Gaede is based on and for the personal gain of one person alone, that being Diana Fruge. She confessed and now she wants to be set free from that … confession. Redemption? I don't think so.

"The state is gonna suggest to you that she was gonna take the blame because she loved Dennis Gaede. Biblical history tells us that Judas loved Jesus, but he betrayed him. He betrayed him for a reason, for 30 pieces of silver. Diana Gaede finally figured out at the end that she had confessed, and she was gonna pay for it, and she looked for a way out and she found it."

Mottinger concluded: "Your job at the end will be to determine whether or not the state has shattered the presumption of innocence and proven their case beyond a reasonable doubt. We will submit to you that it's impossible for them to do that because the only real evidence they have that a crime was committed will come from the lips of Diana Gaede, and that she is not to be believed."

The state's first witness was Sgt. Tamlyn of the Michigan State Police. He described finding Wicks' head, and later his body. Tamlyn also described a receipt for gas and the surveillance video from a Citgo station in Iron

Mountain, which corroborated Fruge's statements that the couple had driven to Gaede's cabin in Powers in the U-Haul truck.

Under cross-examination, Tamlyn told Mottinger that a shoe print, a beer can, a cigarette butt and a puzzle piece were recovered near Wicks' body and analyzed by the Michigan state crime lab. No physical evidence or DNA connected the items to Gaede. The blue fibers that were found on Wicks' body also did not match the blanket from the U-Haul company in Fargo, Tamlyn testified.

Finally, Mottinger elicited testimony from Tamlyn that the handwriting on the Citgo credit card receipt had never been analyzed, so no one knew if it was a match for either Gaede or the real Wicks.

After lunch, Phyllis Allen, the manager of the Citgo station, brought in the actual credit card receipt and testified that she had turned over the surveillance video to the Michigan State Police.

The jury finally got to see the surveillance pictures with the state's third witness, Tony Krogh, the Cass County Sheriff's deputy who had pulled still photos from the Citgo video. After all the anticipation, the pictures themselves were a disappointment. Although the man in them had the same general features and body type as Gaede, their poor quality made it impossible to make a definitive identification.

Neary testified next, describing his brother-in-law as a nice guy who loved music. Neary was followed on the stand by Wicks' former apartment manager, Stacey Paprocki. She talked about the card Wicks had given her, the one with Gaede's phone number on it. The card itself, which she'd turned over to Schoonover, was admitted into evidence.

Then Boening went to find Raychel Fruge, who had to walk into the courtroom alone, without any moral support from her mother. Raychel consistently addressed both Burdick and Mottinger as "Sir." She testified about her trip to Fargo for Christmas, 2001. She testified that Gaede owned a handgun, which she had seen behind the counter at his bait and tackle store. Raychel remained calm and polite on the stand until Burdick neared the end of his questioning. Then she fell apart.

"Before — before let's say January of 2002, how did you feel about Dennis Gaede?" Burdick asked.

"I loved him," Raychel replied, bursting into tears.

"Why is that?" Burdick asked.

"He was a perfect step-dad," the girl replied, losing her composure completely.

Burdick asked the judge's permission to bring her a tissue. Raychel wiped her eyes, and then continued: "He was everything I could have asked for. He gave me anything I wanted or I needed and he was always there for me."

"Did you have any sense from him during that time, before January of 2002, that he was not who he said he was?" Burdick asked after Raychel had composed herself.

"No. I believed him. I didn't think he would ever lie to me. He didn't seem like that type of person."

The state's star witness was next. By the time Fruge was called to the stand, around 2:20 p.m., the courtroom was so crowded that when Burdick leaned back in his chair at the prosecution table, he almost bashed the knees of the spectators in the front row.

Fruge had a new trial wardrobe from the Goodwill thrift store. For only $40, she'd bought several conservative outfits suitable for a state's witness. As she walked to the witness stand for the first time, she wore a black skirt, an orange shirt with matching earrings, and a string of fake pearls. Her makeup was expertly applied.

Fruge testified that Gaede stole Wicks' identity after fleeing Wisconsin to avoid sentencing on felony charges in Monroe County. When Wicks found out, Gaede lured him to North Dakota and killed him, she said.

After Raychel's visit, Fruge and Gaede drove the girl back to Milwaukee, Fruge said. They dropped off Joshua for a visit with his dad and had a holiday dinner with her mom. On December 26, they met up with Wicks. Driving his own car, he followed them back to Fargo. Wicks didn't have a cell phone, so the couple gave him one of theirs to keep in touch on the road.

Fruge next described for the jury the same series of events she had revealed to Schoonover: being awakened by Gaede to find Wicks lying on the floor. He was snoring, she said. "I thought he had done too much partying and had passed out or something," she testified. "I asked Dennis what happened."

Boening braced for Mottinger to object. Under the spousal privilege law, Fruge could testify only to things she had seen. She wasn't allowed to repeat anything Gaede had told her.

But Mottinger didn't speak, and Fruge continued without interruption: "And he said that he shot him." Then Gaede put a plastic garbage bag over Wicks' head because he was still breathing, Fruge said.

"So you immediately called 911?" Boening asked.

"No, I did not."

"You know how 911 works, don't you?"

"Yes."

Boening then asked why Fruge hadn't called for help.

"My mind was just crazy because I was thinking, how would I explain there was a Timothy Wicks on the floor, with Timothy Wicks' car in the driveway and my husband is supposedly Timothy Wicks? So I didn't wind up doing anything," Fruge said.

She described how they cleaned the house. Then McCullough signaled for the afternoon break.

Neary stopped Fruge in the hallway outside the courtroom. So far, she had said everything he had expected, and he grudgingly gave her credit for that. "You're doing a great job," he told her. "Keep it up." Fruge thanked him, then rushed outside for a cigarette.

When court reconvened, Neary and Raychel were sitting next to each other. Back on the stand, Fruge talked about the stop at Fleet Farm and the bizarre road trip she, Gaede and Joshua took with Wicks' corpse in December 2001 and January 2002.

"Everything got loaded in the back of the (U-Haul) truck," she said. "The wardrobe box with the body was attached to the (inside) of the truck with straps so that it wouldn't move around, and after everything was loaded up, we left New Year's Eve night to try to find a place to dispose of the body."

"Okay. How is it that you can remember that it was New Year's Eve night?" Boening asked.

"Because I remember thinking that most people — being the drinker I was at the time — thinking most people are out celebrating the new year and I'm out trying to figure out where to dispose of a body."

The trip included a stop at the Citgo station in Iron Mountain, Michigan, Fruge told the jury. Boening showed her the receipt.

"Whose ... signature appears on that receipt?" he asked.

"It says Timothy Wicks," Fruge answered.

"Did Tim Wicks sign that receipt?" Boening asked.

"No, he did not."

"How do you know that?"

"Because Timothy Wicks wasn't alive."

Fruge then described helping Gaede dump the body. She also talked about the many miles of driving the two did with Joshua, both in their car and in the RV they bought with the money from Wicks' bank account.

At one point, Fruge added a detail to the story that no one in the courtroom had heard before. On the stand, she said she and Gaede had driven through East Troy, the Milwaukee suburb where she grew up, looking for a place to dump Wicks' head and hands.

Boening repeatedly asked Fruge why she was fuzzy about the details, and she repeatedly answered that she was drinking about 12 beers a day at the time, which left her in an alcohol-induced haze.

Boening also asked about the confession Fruge had made to the other inmate in the Nebraska jail.

"Dennis had told me that with his felonies in Wisconsin that if he was convicted of murder, he'd never see daylight again," Fruge testified. "So we concocted a plan. ... He told me if I could convince a jury it was self-defense, I'd be free in eight or nine years and we could be together again."

She wrote a statement to that effect and told the story to several people, she said. "I was in love with him very much," Fruge added, "and I was willing to say that I killed Timothy Wicks so that I could be with him again someday."

The prosecution then introduced as evidence several of the letters Fruge wrote to Gaede from jails in Nebraska and Milwaukee. She then read the letters to the jury. One referred to the statement she wrote about the rape. In another, Fruge wrote that Gaede's previous letter to her had given her a "creepy" feeling. Boening asked her what Gaede's letter had been about. "It was stuff about all these guys that committed grisly crimes and made money on books and stuff," she said. "And he said he could write a book and make money and be one of those guys."

Fruge was still on the stand when court recessed for the day. At dinner that night, she drank heavily.

CHAPTER TWENTY-ONE

With the trains rumbling by the Howard Johnson's, the clang of the Dumpsters being emptied in the early morning hours, and the stress, Fruge didn't get much sleep the night before she faced Mottinger.

The defense attorney showed no mercy, starting off with her shoplifting arrest as a young woman in Florida. It all went downhill from there. Mottinger implied that since Fruge had never mentioned driving around East Troy before, she must have concocted that detail. If she made up that part, he wondered aloud, how reliable could the rest of her testimony be? He pointed out that since she cheated on her first husband with Barranco, she must be a liar. Since she went at Barranco with a knife, she must be violent.

Mottinger then took Fruge through the numerous statements she'd made about killing Wicks because he had raped her.

"Mr. Wicks ever rape you?" Mottinger asked.

"No, he did not."

"But, again, that's not what you told the girls in jail?"

"Correct."

"If somebody raped you, you would be mad, wouldn't you?" Mottinger asked.

"Upset," Fruge answered. Then she continued, surprising everyone in attendance, "I've been raped before."

Mottinger didn't flinch. "And you've already established to the jury that if you get mad at somebody you are capable of picking up a weapon and using it if you think it's appropriate?"

"Yes," Fruge conceded. "I guess I have."

To further prove his point, Mottinger wanted to make Fruge read a portion of another letter she had written to Gaede while they were in jail. In the letter, Fruge wrote that she was more than capable of hurting someone who hurt her. Boening objected, saying it wouldn't be right to read just a portion of a letter out of context.

McCullough ruled in the state's favor, and a grueling ordeal of more than two hours began for Fruge. Mottinger wanted portions of five different letters entered into evidence. According to McCullough's ruling, Fruge would have to read all five in their entirety. The letters went on for many pages of stream-of-consciousness thoughts, some starting one day and continuing hours or days later.

The first was written in Nebraska, where Fruge and Gaede could catch occasional glimpses of each other.

Good morning my dearest baby, it began. *It's 8:00 a.m. I woke up about 4:00 or 4:30, but besides eating breakfast, I've just been laying in bed and praying. Thought about my kids, my mind explodes of all of the laughs and good times I've had with you, how much I love you, how much I would have died to make love to you this morning.*

Fruge flushed as she read that sentence. But it would get worse.

Last but not least, the CD of John Prine has been playing over and over through my mind. ... The (corrections officers) have been giving me envelopes, so I just bought the 34 cent stamps. I don't know why you're paying 37 cents for those envelopes.

I didn't get a letter from you on Friday, so I had to read over the letters I got on Thursday. These smart asses here were teasing me when I was doing haircuts. They said, "Damn, with that write up in the paper we're lucky they let you anywhere close to a scissors or any sharp object for that matter!"

I'm still not sleeping real well. I got about five hours last night. I wrote two (notes to jail officials). One because I found out my lawyers name is Fichter, but I can't get a hold of him, his answering machine is messed up and cuts me off, so I asked if someone could assist me. I told them I needed some photocopies of my statement. It's two

178

pages long. It consists of a short timeline with some blunt descriptions of activity. Everything remains the same.

I love you so much. I'll write to you briefly later. I'm going to make a cup of coffee and jones for a cigarette right now. I hope I can sneak a peek of you today.

The police department wrote back to me. Our motor home is currently at the city impound lot and is being held by Fargo Police Department and FBI. Our vehicle and all our personal belongings would have to be released on one or both of these — by one or both of these agencies.

Oh, Lord, I hope I hear from your mom pretty soon. She should have gotten my letter on Wednesday. She probably didn't get yours until Friday or Saturday. Today is Saturday after dinner. I'm upset because you were like yelling at me to pay attention in that letter and everyone at the table is reading it. I'm sorry but I can't sit and stare at the door for 4½ hours. I was in the middle of a card game. Then I got yelled at for standing by the door at four o'clock. Then the pregnant bitches in here narked on us.

So I'm just — I'm going for now and gonna mail it. There are too many snitches over here! I didn't get the part in your letter where it says, "Have you discovered (sic) your sex life with anyone? I guess you're safe in there. You have a captive audience. You've got the point." I don't know what that means. Anyway, no, I didn't get the point. Explain to me. And I've only discussed our sex life a little, just with my roommate and she only does dark meat so I think I'm safe.

Good morning my love. I've been up here for hours thinking about you. I was wishing I could wake up and feel you kissing my neck and my ears, moving my hands —

Fruge abruptly stopped reading. "I'm not going to go into that," she said.

"You're gonna have to read it, ma'am," McCullough admonished.

Fruge gave him a mortified look, then continued: ... *moving your hands from my nipples down to my hip bones*

179

and all the way — the way you do that so sexy! From there I give you pleasure and away we go. What a great fantasy!

After a few more minutes of reading, Fruge came to the part of the letter Mottinger wanted the jurors to hear.

When the counselor asked that I was — if I was sure I wasn't going to hurt myself I said, "No I just think about hurting other people that hurt me."

After reading four letters, Fruge's nerves were shot. Mottinger handed her another. "Oh, Jesus," she muttered. "How many of these am I gonna have to read?"

"Ms. Fruge, you don't want the jury to hear what you wrote in these letters?" Mottinger asked after the fifth letter had been entered into evidence.

"No, I just — it's quite personal," she replied. "That's all. A lot of it."

Mottinger was unsympathetic: "Go ahead and read it." He was waiting for the bombshell, and Fruge got to it soon enough.

I saw the Catholic priest today, she read. *I confessed my sins, all of them, the big one. I had to do penance obviously. He told me that God forgives me. I was struggling with acceptance of God's forgiveness. I have prayed for us months but never knew if we would be forgiven. I read in a pamphlet the only way God will allow us into heaven is if we confess our sins and by faith accept Jesus Christ. After the church service I asked Father John, "How do you know if God has forgiven you for the sins that you confessed?" He explained that in our Catholic religion it's confession, which I knew. So I asked how I go about doing that here, and he said he would listen to my confession right now.*

It was a very hard thing to do. I was crying. I was embarrassed. Not only have I asked for forgiveness for my major sins, but the small ones as well. I haven't been to confession since I found out I was pregnant with Joshua. I asked God to forgive me for getting pregnant out of wedlock. I sure feel a lot easier about everything now. My pen-

ance was 15 Our Father's 15 Hail Mary's and to pray for my family to get through this.

I went straight to my room and on my knees right in front of Biggie I prayed and begged for God's forgiveness. I felt like a huge cloud was lifted from me when Father John told me that God has forgiven me. I will tell you that it was extremely difficult to confess to a human being, even if he was of the cloth. I feel like I'm stronger now and that I can go on instead of the battle of not knowing if I'll go to heaven. Keep praying, sweetheart, and God will bring us back together one day.

In the letter, the description of Fruge's confession was followed by another graphic sexual fantasy, which she was again forced to read aloud. When Fruge had finished reading, Mottinger asked, "Is the big one you talked to the Catholic priest about the murder of Timothy Wicks?"

"Yes, it is."

"If you didn't kill him, what was there to confess for?" the lawyer asked.

"Because I was responsible for not calling 911, and I was responsible for seeing the man be dismembered and help dispose of the body," she answered.

"So that was your great consternation and that's what you were so afraid of?" Mottinger asked skeptically.

"Yes," Fruge answered. "It was."

Boening sensed that Mottinger's strategy had backfired. Instead of painting Fruge as a cold-hearted killer or even a rape victim, she came across as a somewhat pathetic figure, blinded by love. Boening had the feeling the letters had earned Fruge sympathy with the jury.

The assistant state's attorney went easy on Fruge when he questioned her again, emphasizing that the letters were truthful and showed how much she had loved Gaede when she wrote them.

Fruge remained on the stand until lunchtime. She was back there for the afternoon session, which started a little late because one of the jurors had gotten into a fender bender on the corner on the way back to the courthouse after lunch.

By 1:40 p.m., Fruge was finally done testifying. McCullough refused to release her from her subpoena, however, so she returned to the law library. As she left the courtroom, Burdick asked McCullough if they could bring in a fan to ease the stifling heat. McCullough said no, and Burdick sipped from a bottle of Dasani water, ignoring the pitcher of tap water and paper cups on the prosecution table.

The afternoon's testimony began with the security director of M&I Bank presenting the evidence that would have been used in Milwaukee County's botched forgery case: withdrawal slips, photos, and video from the bank's security cameras as Gaede took money out of Wicks' account.

Schoonover took the stand next, identifying Gaede in the bank photos and walking the jury through his portion of the investigation. On cross-examination, Mottinger was only interested in the call Schoonover had received from Wicks' longtime friend Susanna Stevens, a call Schoonover had deemed insignificant at the time. Mottinger introduced Schoonover's report of the conversation into evidence. It said Stevens claimed to have seen Wicks at Vic's Clique on December 28. According to Fruge's version of events, Wicks was already dead by then.

Schoonover assumed Stevens had been mistaken about the date, and he told Boening as much on cross-examination. Unfortunately for Mottinger, no one could ask Stevens if she was sure she'd seen Wicks. The defense attorney would have subpoenaed her, but he hadn't been able to find her.

Jeff Paridon and Gene Maxwell's company, Compressed Air Technologies, had gone belly up by the time the trial rolled around. As Paridon took the stand, he told the jury, "I do not work at this time." Maxwell described himself as "independently employed." The two men believed Gaede's embezzlement from their company, as well as the computer problems they had experienced while Gaede was driving around the country shortly after Christmas, had led to Compressed Air's demise. By the time Gaede went to trial, their civil suit against the Spherion employment agency for recommending him as a bookkeeper was pending.

Paridon and Maxwell's testimony was important to corroborate the fact that Gaede had been living as Wicks. Paridon testified about the third person he had seen in the Z-24 with Gaede and Fruge, whom the jurors could safely assume was Wicks. Paridon also testified about Gaede's phone call asking to use the Bobcat, which backed up Fruge's story that Gaede had first tried to bury Wicks' body in their yard in Gardner.

Paridon also had a few opinions about Gaede, the con man. "He's a very likeable guy," Paridon said of his former bookkeeper. "He's a very convincing guy when he wants to be. ... We could have a conversation right now and you could sit down with him and he could tell you that it was pitch black outside and you'd have to go out and verify it for yourself that it was indeed daylight. He was very, very good."

CHAPTER TWENTY-TWO

When Detective Paul Lies of the Fargo Police Department sprayed the kitchen floor of the Gardner farmhouse with Luminol, a chemical designed to detect traces of blood, the linoleum lit up like a Christmas tree. The reaction was the closest thing prosecutors had to physical evidence of Wicks' murder.

The Luminol took center stage as Boening questioned Lies on the witness stand during the fourth day of Gaede's trial. "When you used it in the kitchen, did anything unusual happen?" Boening asked.

"The floor glowed," Lies replied. Later, he elaborated: "Pretty much the whole floor."

Boening wanted to be sure he made his point. "You don't know if it glowed more than any Luminol has glowed ever in the world, but in your experience you saw more Luminol glowing than you've ever seen on another crime scene?" he asked.

Lies agreed.

Then Boening switched topics. He never asked Lies why the floor was glowing so much. Had someone dumped a bucket of blood there? That didn't seem consistent with Fruge's statement about a small spot of blood under Wicks' head. Was Wicks actually dismembered in the Gardner kitchen? But even that wouldn't explain a huge amount of blood in the kitchen, since Wicks' body had been frozen before his head and hands were removed.

Mottinger didn't clarify the point when he got his turn to question Lies. "Now as I understand it when you used Luminol, the entire floor reacted in a positive manner?"

Lies agreed and repeated that he had never seen anything like that before.

"Can't really explain it either?" Mottinger asked.

"I have — I have a theory as to why it happened, yes," Lies replied. But the jurors would never hear Lies' theory because Mottinger never asked about it.

Four more witnesses testified for several hours before the jurors heard anything else about the Luminol. Kevin Liedhal, manager of the U-Haul rental shop, brought in the receipts of Gaede's transactions and told the jurors that, yes, a body would fit into a couple of wardrobe boxes. Richard Schmidt of United Rentals brought in a receipt for a backhoe rented under the name Tim Wicks on a Saturday that had been returned to the parking lot — not checked in face-to-face — by Monday.

Cass County Sheriff's Deputy Patricia Wasmuth talked about getting a call from Paridon at the Gardner farmhouse and breaking in, only to find nobody there. Rick Majerus detailed the extensive efforts he and other investigators made in their search for physical evidence of the murder, then conceded they found none.

Finally, Hope Olson of the state crime lab in Bismarck cleared up the issue of the Luminol. Blood wasn't the only thing that could cause the chemical to glow, she testified. Another common culprit was bleach. Even diluted bleach, found in a household product like Clorox Clean-Up, would be enough to make the Luminol react, she said.

Olson also testified about trying to tie Wicks' murder to the Gardner farmhouse. She was unsuccessful with every attempt, and Mottinger used her testimony to pound home the fact that there was no forensic evidence at all that implicated Gaede.

When Olson had finished answering questions, the prosecution was done calling witnesses. Mottinger made the standard defense argument that Gaede should be immediately acquitted because the state had not proven its case. McCullough quickly denied the motion.

Mottinger first called Sherri Cotter, the corrections officer from Nebraska who showed Fruge the newspaper article at the jail. She testified that Fruge had confessed to the crime.

Next, the defense lawyer called FBI Special Agent John Dalziel. Less buttoned-down than most federal agents, Dalziel had a shaved head, moustache, and scruffy beard. He was a seasoned witness, among only a few North Dakota officers who didn't mispronounce Schoonover's hometown of Hales Corners as "Hales Corner." Dalziel didn't ramble, and he was careful to answer exactly what he was asked. Mottinger's intent in calling Dalziel was to hammer home, again, the fact that there was no physical evidence tying Gaede to Wicks' murder.

On cross examination, Boening asked if it was possible for someone to commit a crime without leaving trace evidence behind. Dalziel confirmed it was. It wouldn't be hard, Dalziel said, for someone like himself, someone trained in law enforcement, to clean up a crime scene completely.

"What is your reaction to the fact that no trace evidence was found in this case? How can you explain that?" Boening asked.

"Mr. Gaede was a police officer at one point," Dalziel answered matter-of-factly. Most people involved in the case already knew about Gaede's history in law enforcement. But to the jurors, Dalziel's simple statement was a bombshell. Boening didn't ask Dalziel to elaborate too much. His point had been made.

Mottinger worried that Dalziel's statement was perhaps the final nail in Gaede's coffin.

Since Mottinger hadn't been able to locate Susanna Stevens, only Gaede remained on Mottinger's witness list.

Boening was almost certain Gaede would testify and hoped the defendant would. The prosecution's entire trial strategy had been designed to force him to do so. Burdick and Boening had been careful not to elicit too much detail about Gaede's statements to law enforcement from the officers who had testified — even those statements that

187

tended to show Gaede was guilty. That way, Mottinger couldn't cross examine them about Gaede's other statements — the ones where he protested that he hadn't killed Wicks. The savvy defense lawyer had been known to use that strategy in other cases. In this trial, Boening and Burdick wouldn't let it happen. Unless Gaede took the stand, the prosecutors were determined that jurors wouldn't hear his denials of the crime.

If Gaede did decide to testify, Boening was ready for him. Gaede was a good talker. Good enough, perhaps, to create reasonable doubt in the minds of the jurors. On cross-examination, though, Boening thought he could point out enough inconsistencies to prove Gaede wasn't credible.

Boening and Burdick expected that Gaede would try to pin the crime on Fruge. In one of his talks with police, he'd hinted that she probably called Barranco to help dispose of Wicks' body. If he did, the prosecution was ready for that, too. Barranco had been flown in from Milwaukee the night before in case he was needed for rebuttal.

"Call your next witness, Mr. Mottinger," McCullough instructed.

"Defense rests," Mottinger replied.

Boening was stunned.

Mottinger was glad he'd thrown his rival for a loop. He knew Boening had spent inordinate amounts of time preparing to cross-examine Gaede. That was one of the reasons Mottinger chose not to call him. It was a deviation from his general practice. Usually, a likeable defendant who claimed he didn't do it would take the stand. With Gaede, though, it was too risky. Because of his checkered past, it would be hard to make the jury believe he was telling the truth.

It hadn't been a difficult decision. Fargo was such a small town that the lawyers all knew each other's strengths. One of Boening's was cross-examination. He would be sure to get in anything that could damage Gaede's credibility, including his past identity thefts in Canada and his lengthy criminal record. In a case like this, where it was difficult for the prosecution to prove jurisdiction, let alone the defendant's guilt, there was nothing to gain by putting Gaede on the stand, Mottinger decided.

Boening didn't have time to process the fact that Gaede wouldn't testify. McCullough immediately asked him if he wanted to recall any witnesses.

"The state recalls Sherri Cotter," Boening replied.

It's a cardinal rule of litigation not to ask a witness a question unless you're reasonably sure of what she's going to say. Boening was about to break the rule. The assistant state's attorney asked Cotter if she had shown Gaede the same newspaper article she had shown Fruge. She had. In answer to Boening's questions, Cotter said Gaede was calm and didn't ask any questions about the murder charges against him, nor did he implicate Fruge. Boening continued: "Did you find that unusual as part of your observation of — of inmates who are brought into jail that when you confront them with a newspaper article alleging that they're involved in a murder, you confront them with that, that they have no reaction to that?" Cotter's answer was matter-of-fact: "His only reaction was that he didn't commit the crime."

Boening couldn't believe he had been so stupid. Just like that, he'd almost blown his entire trial strategy. Gaede had refused to testify, yet almost the last piece of evidence jurors heard during the trial was his denial of the crime.

That night Mottinger worked on his closing argument for a couple of hours, then went to the jail to see his client. Mottinger told Gaede that during closing arguments, he planned to admit that Gaede had committed a host of crimes, from embezzlement to credit card fraud. Mottinger believed that in order for the jury to believe him, he would have to admit the strengths of the state's case and concede Gaede's shortcomings. If he tried to refute the identity theft, the trip to Fleet Farm, the things that were obviously provable, Mottinger felt he would lose credibility with the jury.

Gaede didn't like the idea. He looked at his lawyer across the table in the jail visiting room as if Mottinger were crazy. Mottinger was convinced, though, that his strategy would work. The proof of the lesser crimes was so strong that proof of the murder was nonexistent by comparison. When Mottinger finally headed home, darkness was falling. Burdick's car was still in the courthouse parking lot.

*   *   *

Closing arguments began on Friday morning. Burdick had his say first.

"To look at the defendant you might not think of him as a runner, but that's exactly what he is," Burdick began. "He's running from his own reality. When he was convicted in Wisconsin, he ran because he was terrified of going to jail, and to assist him in that flight, he ran from his own identity and he took Timothy Wicks'.

"And when he was here, he then ran from his employer when they discovered his embezzlement and fraud. And when Timothy Wicks discovered that somebody was using his identity, the defendant ran right over Timothy Wicks' life and he extinguished it with a shot to the head. And when he had done that … he took Timothy Wicks' credit card and he ran with it and he bought the things that he tried to use and in fact did use to disguise, bury, and dispose of Timothy Wicks' body.

"And he also ran through $17,000 of Timothy Wicks' savings, then he ran. He ran around the countryside trying to avoid accountability for his reality, but finally he was captured. That was in early March.

"He's a runner. Do you know what today is? Today is the day that you get to bring his run from reality to an end."

190

Burdick then used a timeline to guide the jurors though the prosecution's version of events: the fake drumming gig in Canada, the murder in Gardner, the rental of the U-Haul and the backhoe, the road trip to dispose of the body.

"There he is," Burdick said later, pointing to Gaede. "He's wanted on convictions. This guy, this sterling citizen, betrays his friend, Timothy Wicks, by taking his identity but that's not enough. It doesn't get him what he needs. He gets discovered. He can't continue his charade, so what does he do? Sterling citizen takes the next step and he kills the source of his problem.

"And isn't that enough? No, because he's got to do something with the body. So what does he do? He runs. And if that's not enough, because it isn't — because he gets caught, he does one other thing. He blames his wife. He shifts the blame to Diana Fruge.

"So you gotta ask yourself the question because I know I did. Why? Why would Diana say yes to this?

"... You can see, can't you, that there can be times when you would do almost anything to protect someone you love. And did Diana Fruge love Gaede? How can you miss it? We heard a little bit more in those letters than we all wanted to hear, but the one theme that you heard throughout those letters was her undying love for him. I love you. I love you. I love you.

"Love is the answer here to the question why would she be willing to accept a shifting of the blame for this murder to herself from him. ... He told her that if he got caught for this crime, he'd go away for life. I mean, this isn't a 30-day sentence for a DUI. He would go away for life."

Burdick adopted Gaede's persona: "Honey, I am going to go away for life if I get caught for this. But you — because I know these things, honey, because ... I was a cop. I know these things. You, you can claim self-defense. Let's say he raped you and you tried to defend yourself and you shot him that way. Why, if you go to jail, if you go to jail maybe it'll only be eight or nine years. What's that in comparison to life, my love, my sweet? What comparison is that? And she ... bought it. She bought the argument because love is the answer."

Burdick ended with a humble request to the 12 men and women who would decide Gaede's fate. "In the end, this is what I ask you to do. I ask you to go into the jury deliberation room, look at all the evidence. ... Recall the testimony that you heard from the witness stand. Mull it over. Talk it through, but when you're done ... come back into this room and tell that man, that running man, that he may run but he can't hide from his own reality."

After a 40-minute break, it was Mottinger's turn. Almost immediately, the defense attorney pounced on Boening's misstep, reminding the jury that Gaede had denied the crime to Sherri Cotter, just as he had denied it by formally pleading not guilty to the murder charge. There was no physical evidence in the Gardner home, Mottinger repeated. None in the U-Haul where a body had allegedly been dismembered. None in Gaede's Michigan cabin.

Mottinger's closing argument was rife with Biblical imagery. Again, he talked about how Fruge, like Judas, helped the authorities end a logjam and get their man. He characterized Fruge as a sinner, saying she had no more right to be believed than Gaede.

"Ask yourself this," he instructed the jury. "Why is (Burdick's) sinner to be believed and why is mine to be condemned? And, yes, Dennis Gaede is mine. He's my responsibility. He has been from the day I took on his case, was asked to represent him, and he's gonna be my responsibility throughout the remainder of this case. So why is his sinner to be accepted and mine to be condemned? I can't answer that. I just can't answer that."

Fruge's timeline was also a problem, Mottinger said. She said the murder was December 28, yet Susanna

Stevens had told Schoonover she saw Wicks that day, back in Wisconsin.

"Do you remember a few days ago I mentioned that Harry Truman parable when I was up here?" Mottinger asked, alluding again to his opening statement. "He had mentioned one time that whenever you hear somebody praying too loud in the front yard, you better run out back and make sure the smokehouse is locked. The application and relevance of that analogy to this case and what you've heard in this room over the past few days should by now be absolutely crystal clear to you. And, no, I'm not suggesting that the folks over at that table are trying to steal something when you aren't looking.

"But rather what I'm suggesting is that they're trying to distract you from the real issues in front of you and have you convict Dennis Gaede of a murder because of all the other non-related, non-relevant, bad acts that they think they can prove or maybe they'd even prove. They can prove he embezzled money. They got a conviction. They can probably prove he took money out of Tim Wicks' account. You saw the pictures. They can probably prove he used Tim Wicks' credit card. You saw the stuff from Fleet Farm. They can prove a lot of those things. We're not going to sit here and argue about things that they can prove. The one thing they cannot, however, prove is that a murder was committed in this county and that Tim Wicks was murdered here. They just can't prove it."

Mottinger then returned to his humble, folksy approach. "I told you a little earlier I wished I was a better lawyer," he said. "I meant it then and I really mean it now. I only hope I can measure up. I stand here in front of you, the last thing between Dennis Gaede and them. Again, I can only hope I'm up to that task because if I fail on behalf of Dennis Gaede, I will be very disappointed in myself to say the least.

"Why? Because I'm entirely convinced that there's just not enough evidence that's been presented to prove this case beyond a reasonable doubt. They have not been able to do it. It's really that simple. They can hint at it. They can suggest it. They can say he might have done it. They can say he probably did it. They can say that he was somehow involved in it. But you know what? They cannot prove it. Proof by mere conjecture alone is never enough."

Mottinger told the jurors that Fruge, like the boy who cried wolf, was not to be believed. The prosecution's argument that Fruge had helped Gaede cover up the murder out of love worked just as well in reverse, Mottinger said. Fruge had confessed to the crime. Maybe Gaede's only crime was loving her so much that *he* tried to help *her* cover it up.

"You are going to find Dennis Gaede not guilty not because you necessarily want him to be not guilty, but because that's exactly what he is," Mottinger instructed the jurors. "And he is not guilty because they just don't have the evidence to prove it.

"In closing I simply want to say that I am unapologetically and unequivocally an advocate for Dennis Gaede. I have done my best over the course of the last few days to represent him and his interests. If in the course of that representation I've gone too far, I've offended you, made you mad, please hold these sins and transgressions against me, not against Dennis Gaede.

"Ladies and gentlemen, my work here is done. Your difficult work is yet to begin. May you do it well. ... Both Dennis and I are absolutely convinced that you are going to do the very, very best job that you can. That's all any of us can ask for. Thank you."

After a brief rebuttal argument from Burdick, Gaede's fate was in the hands of the jury.

CHAPTER TWENTY-THREE

For Burdick, the most difficult part of any trial was the end, and Gaede's was no exception. Once the testimony was over, the arguments done, the prosecutor was left feeling helpless. Once the case was in the hands of the jury, Burdick no longer had any power over the outcome of the case. No control.

Mottinger focused on not second-guessing himself. If he had made mistakes, there was no going back now. He felt he had done his best. Now he hoped his best had been good enough to save his client. There was nothing left to do but wait.

Mottinger was surprised at how little time it took. Three and a half hours after starting their deliberations, the jury returned. The defense lawyer was feeling pretty confident.

The jury forewoman, Starla Siewert, handed the verdict form to the bailiff. Tears welled in her eyes. The clerk's hands and her voice shook as she read the document aloud.

The preamble seemed to go on forever: "In District Court, County of Cass, State of North Dakota. State of North Dakota, plaintiff, versus Dennis James Gaede, defendant. Verdict, criminal No. 09-05-K-2878. We, the jury duly impaneled and sworn in the above-entitled action, do find the defendant, Dennis James Gaede, guilty of the crime of murder as charged in the Information. Dated at Fargo, North Dakota, this 7th day of April, 2006."

Mottinger tried not to betray his feelings on his face. Shit. He never should have called John Dalziel.

A look of total disbelief passed across the Gaede's face as the judge polled the jurors, making sure each one agreed with the guilty verdict.

Fruge stood, lips pursed, and tried not to cry as her ex-husband was led away. Her first thought was, "Thank God." Thank God it was over. Thank God Gaede would never get the opportunity to hurt her or her children. Thank God the jurors hadn't believed all the lies Mottinger had tried to sell them.

From the beginning of their deliberations, all the jurors were pretty much on the same page about what their verdict would be. They had gotten to know Tim Wicks pretty well through Neary's testimony, and they didn't believe he was the type of guy who would rape a friend's wife. More importantly, all of the circumstantial evidence fit: Paprocki's testimony about Wicks loading his drums into his car; Gaede's rental of the backhoe, then the U-Haul truck; Wicks' credit card being used in Fargo, then Michigan.

When the FBI's Dalziel revealed that Gaede had once been a police officer, any reasonable doubt about the lack of physical evidence disappeared. It made perfect sense that Gaede, trained in the type of evidence cops look for, had cleaned up so thoroughly that all the bleach on the kitchen floor made the Luminol glow.

Some of the jurors had been confused about Fruge's statement that Wicks was breathing, making snoring noises, after being shot in the head. Siewert set them straight. She was a nurse, and she'd seen that kind of thing in the emergency room. Siewert had tried to put herself in Fruge's place in other ways, too. Siewert imagined Fruge, helpless, knowing the whole situation was wrong but powerless to stop it. She simply stood by as the hole she was in got deeper and deeper until it seemed there was no way out.

The jurors had paid attention to Gaede, even though he didn't take the stand. At several points during the trial, after the prosecution had proven something particularly incriminating, he had turned beet red, and more than one of the jurors noticed.

They dismissed Susanna Stevens' report that she'd seen Wicks in Wisconsin on December 28 as a red herring. Wicks' car was definitely in Fargo that day. Both Jeff Paridon from Compressed Air and the sheriff's deputy who

196

helped break into the Gardner farmhouse saw it. If Wicks' car was in Fargo, there was no way he was back in Wisconsin.

Even Cotter's testimony, which had so worried Boening, turned out to be helpful to the prosecution. The jurors had a theory about why Gaede didn't react when Cotter showed him the newspaper article. "You know why he had no reaction?" Siewert asked. "He's a damn psychopath."

Burdick and Boening were on cloud nine as they faced the throng of television cameras. Burdick admitted to the reporters that he would have liked more evidence against Gaede. He credited both his assistant prosecutor and all the cops in three states for sticking with him for more than three years. "They didn't give up on it. They worked until we knew everything we could know," he said. "Tim Wicks was . . . a nice guy who did nothing to earn what happened to him. He was just an unfortunate victim of Dennis Gaede." Burdick was hopeful that the guilty verdict would bring a measure of relief and a sense of justice to Wicks' family.

Despite the verdict, Mottinger felt it had been the right decision to keep Gaede off the witness stand. "This was a very interesting case," he told the reporters. "We did the best we could, but unfortunately for Mr. Gaede, it wasn't good enough." Gaede would almost certainly appeal, Mottinger said.

Schoonover hadn't stuck around to wait for the verdict. By the time Gaede was shackled and taken back to jail, the detective was on his way back to Wisconsin. He had taken a break from driving and was in a store when his cell phone rang, a reporter with news of the verdict. Schoonover was happy to provide a few quotes. "The truth always wins out in the end," he said. "It took a long time, but Tim finally got justice."

Immediately, he called Neary, who was back at work at his tool and die company in suburban Milwaukee. "I have great news," the detective began.

"They put the SOB away, didn't they?" Neary asked as the endorphins flooded his bloodstream and he was overcome with joy.

"First degree intentional homicide," Schoonover confirmed. For the Wisconsin detective, it was a satisfying culmination to the most challenging and most frustrating case of his career.

*   *   *

Not quite three months after his trial, Gaede was back in McCullough's Fargo courtroom for sentencing. In North Dakota, the maximum penalty for murder is life in prison without the possibility of parole. That sentence, however, is not mandatory. Ultimately, it was up to McCullough to decide when, or if, Gaede would ever be free again.

Neither Wicks' family, nor his friends, nor Schoonover made the trip from Wisconsin this time. Wicks' loved ones had sent letters to the judge, but on this balmy June Thursday, Burdick alone would speak aloud for the victim.

"The road to death, an untimely death, fans out in several directions," the prosecutor began. "There could be accident, illness, maybe a stupid act in the heat of the moment, but a premeditated murder, now that's the most frightening because it gives us a terrible peek into the cold and callous heart of some people, and this is just such a case. The tragic end that came for Timothy Wicks came not in one moment and it came not in a single act, but it was a culmination of a series of acts by the defendant."

Much of the evidence during Gaede's trial, Burdick reminded the judge, pointed to a sophisticated plan and an extended timeline for the crime. The state's attorney called

198

the dismemberment of Wicks' body and its disposal around the Midwest "the ultimate indignity." If Gaede were to be released, Burdick said, it was quite likely that the defendant would commit another crime.

"The state knows of nothing that mitigates the defendant's behavior in this case," Burdick concluded. "It knows of nothing that softens the obvious callousness of his heart. It knows of no reason why the state should recommend anything less than everything the law will allow."

Earlier that morning, Gaede had asked Mottinger to file an appeal. As soon as it was Mottinger's turn to speak, he told McCullough about that decision. It put both Mottinger and his client in a difficult position. At sentencing, judges tend to be more lenient when defendants admit what they have done and apologize. In legal parlance, it's called "accepting responsibility." Gaede wasn't doing it.

Nonetheless, where Burdick had found no mitigating circumstances, Mottinger saw several. Gaede was in poor health, an overweight man with diabetes. The lack of exercise and nutrition in prison would not be kind to him, and he would probably not live to a ripe old age. Mottinger conceded that Gaede had a criminal record, but pointed out that none of those past crimes were violent. If Gaede had really been so cold and calculating, Mottinger said, he certainly would have done away with Fruge before she could give the testimony that would bury him.

In North Dakota, a sentence of life with the possibility of parole translated to 30 years (25 if the defendant behaved himself in prison) before the state's pardon board would consider release. That is the sentence Mottinger requested on Gaede's behalf.

"I know that Dennis would like me to argue for something less than that, but I honestly believe we have to be realistic," Mottinger said. "It would be unfair of me, and I indicated this to Dennis earlier this week, to suggest the court do something that in all likelihood the court would not be in a position to do."

Mottinger knew the odds of McCullough allowing Gaede a chance at parole were slim. He had been convicted of a heinous crime, and he had a criminal record. In Mottinger's view, though, no one was beyond redemption. He made an attempt to convince McCullough that Gaede should have a chance to see freedom again.

"Twenty-five years would put Mr. Gaede in his ... mid-to-late 60s before he was eligible for release," Mottinger said. "At that point I think all of the concerns addressed by Mr. Burdick to this court would probably be moot, and at that point Mr. Gaede would present no further risk to anybody. To suggest that a life sentence (with parole) is somehow lenient is ludicrous. On the other hand, a life sentence does give Mr. Gaede some hope for the future, assuming that the appeal is not successful, and perhaps would serve to motivate him to do whatever good he can do while incarcerated."

When Mottinger was finished, McCullough heard directly from Gaede for the first time. Dressed in orange jail coveralls, the defendant stood to read from a sheet of paper.

"Your Honor, in my 42 years, I never thought that I would be standing in a court moments away from having the rest of my life handed to me.

"Timothy Wicks, the victim in this case, and I shared a love for music and we also shared many dreams for the future. Those dreams were shattered in January of 2002 when my ex-wife, Diana Fruge, revealed to me her vile act, one that only a monster could commit.

"In a role that the actor John Malkovich once played, he said, 'We can't have monsters roaming the countryside now, can we?' Well, Mr. Burdick and Mr. Boening would like the world to believe that I am in fact that monster, but in truth the man standing before you is not a monster. However, the real one still does roam the countryside.

200

"A few days ago I read the victim impact statement that the Wicks family wrote. We've all lost loved ones in our lives ... but to lose one in such a macabre manner is nothing short ... of heartbreaking. Six years ago, I lost a family member, too, in a senseless murder. It hurts everyone and keeps on hurting. My deepest sympathy goes out to the Wicks family. This, too, is a senseless murder. They lost a family member and I lost a friend.

"When this trial started," Gaede continued, "I thought the truth would finally come out, but it didn't. Then we saw a lamia, a female demon, take the witness stand. Then she used every deceptive tactic that she knows to save herself and sway the court into believing lies that she professed to be the truth. That demon, Diana Fruge, is responsible for the murder of Timothy Wicks. She may be sending me to prison today, but my conscience is clear that I'm not a murderer.

"Your Honor, this case in my eyes is a manifest injustice. Everyone would like to believe that this is poetic justice, but it is clearly a miscarriage. I don't blame Mr. Burdick, Mr. Boening, Captain Majerus, Special Agent Dalziel or even the jury for what has happened. They fell prey to the deception just like I did."

It was impossible not to notice that Schoonover's name was conspicuously absent from the list of people Gaede held blameless.

He continued: "However, Mr. Mottinger has given me hope that at least two of these gentlemen saw through the deception during my trial. That's the first step in righting this wrong, and I want them to know that ... I'm going to help them take that next step.

"Your Honor, I know that you have a job to do today and, frankly, based on the heinous nature of this crime, I'm expecting the worst sentence possible. However, I will let the court know that we will be visiting this case again. Because one way or the other, the truth is going to be heard.

201

"When Mr. Mottinger made his opening argument during the trial, he ironically referenced the story of Judas' betrayal of Jesus. Jesus, too, was convicted of a crime that he was innocent of. That was 2,000 years ago, and many people still can't see the obvious truth in his case, either. We will, though, in this case because I know that God is on my side and with his help and divine intervention, the true murderess who committed this heinous act will be brought to justice.

"Your Honor, I am not a violent offender and I pose no danger to anyone. My past record will reflect that. I have made a few mistakes, but the last four years in prison corrected them and they will never happen again.

"In this case, I just fell in love with the wrong person, and now two innocent men are paying for it, Tim Wicks and me. I will accept whatever punishment this court hands down, but I want everyone to know that I did not commit this murder. Thank you."

McCullough wasn't buying it. Before the sentencing hearing, he had reviewed the transcript of Fruge's statement to the FBI, and he accepted it as true.

McCullough called Fruge "admittedly a pathetic figure in this sad scenario," but not the responsible party.

"Mr. Gaede needed Ms. Fruge as someone on whom he could pin the blame for this crime," the judge said. "She was just as much a tool in the commission of this crime as the saw he used to cut off (Wicks') head and hands."

McCullough did agree with a statement Gaede had made in writing before the sentencing: It took someone with a cold and evil heart to kill Wicks. But that person, McCullough said, was Gaede, not Fruge. "Mr. Gaede's pathetic statement that he took no part in the killing or disposal of the body is ludicrously inconsistent with the facts proven at trial," McCullough finished. No one was surprised when the judge sentenced Gaede to life without the possibility of parole.

EPILOGUE

Dennis Gaede appealed his conviction and sentence to North Dakota's Supreme Court. He said Mottinger's representation had constituted a miscarriage of justice. When Fruge testified about things discussed within their marriage, Mottinger should have objected, Gaede's new attorney said. When Sherri Cotter talked about Gaede's reaction to the newspaper article, Mottinger should have objected again. Gaede also argued that he had wanted to testify at the trial, but Mottinger wouldn't let him.

In July 2007, the Supreme Court dismissed all of those arguments and upheld the guilty verdict and life sentence.

Beth Neary can't use Clorox Clean-Up anymore without thinking about her brother's blood on the kitchen floor of a North Dakota farmhouse. Every Christmas, there's a hint of melancholy as the family realizes they're spending another holiday without Tim. When Beth wants to remember, she plays one of her brother's favorite albums: "A Question of Balance," by the Moody Blues.

In his own basement music studio, Tom Neary has hung a poster he recovered from Wicks' apartment. It's a picture of Buddy Rich playing at the International Jazz Festival. Neary doesn't know if Tim attended, but he hopes his brother-in-law was there, happy, grooving to the music.

Nowadays when Koehler and the rest of Wicks' pals want to raise a glass to their friend, they go to Kokopelli's, where Wicks sometimes played on Sunday nights.

Gerry Boettcher has often related an experience he is sure was a message from beyond the grave. On the day Wicks disappeared, before anyone knew his fate, Boettcher was driving down Manitoba Avenue in Milwaukee when he spotted a set of drums on the side of the road. They weren't exactly like Wicks', but Boettcher knew his friend would like them. He brought the drums home and set them up in the basement so Wicks could check them out when he came back to town.

The drums were still there a few weeks later, after Boettcher learned of Wicks' death. Rock music with a strong bass line blasted from the stereo. Boettcher was surprised when he also heard pounding on his bedroom floor, like someone was banging on the ceiling of the basement below.

Boettcher turned off the music, but the thumping continued. He went down the stairs. The drums were still. Boettcher saw no one in the basement, but he is convinced Wicks was there.

Printed in the United States
124060LV00001B/2/P

9 781932 542363